"Jimmy Agan's *The Imitation*
about more than imitation.
tion to Christ is a consequence of his grace toward us, and the whole work resonates with the sweetness and clarity of one who himself serves Christ in the grateful radiance of the gospel profoundly grasped."

—**Bryan Chapell**, President Emeritus, Covenant Theological Seminary; Senior Pastor, Grace Presbyterian Church (PCA), Peoria, Illinois

"Imitation of Christ—a topic that is of profound importance, but has nonetheless been besieged by theological questions among well-intentioned scholars, is here presented in a way that is both deeply rooted in the pages of the New Testament and yet also eminently accessible to the contemporary reader. This is the work of a scholar who is also a convinced and gifted communicator."

—**Andrew Clarke**, Senior Lecturer, Divinity and Religious Studies, King's College, University of Aberdeen

"Is it appropriate for Christians to imitate Christ, or does this undermine the uniqueness of Christ's work? Dr. Agan addresses this important question from the Gospel of Luke by providing biblical rationale and interpretive guidelines for imitating Christ in four key respects. Here is a work of applied theology that will encourage you to follow more closely in the footsteps of our Lord, while continually relying on his grace in the gospel."

—**Brandon D. Crowe**, Assistant Professor of New Testament, Westminster Theological Seminary

"As Christians, we are called to imitate Jesus, which we cannot do in our own strength—yet Jesus is not only a model, but also the source that enables us to be like him. C. D. 'Jimmy' Agan has written an excellent work on the Gospel according to Luke that is suffused with the challenge to imitate Jesus, but not in the manner of those who see Jesus only as a role model or of those who try to see everything as being all of grace to an extreme. Agan has placed this topic of 'servant example' around Luke 6:40: the disciple is to be like his teacher. In the historically redemptive context, it becomes clear by Jesus' saving work on our behalf that he enables us to be like him. Agan has given us a great resource for preaching and teaching, and the layperson will also benefit from his writing. I was personally humbled and challenged as I read the manuscript. I challenge each preacher to consider reading this volume and then committing to using it to teach the Gospel according to Luke. This book will be a tremendous alternative to so much superficiality and triviality associated with being a kingdom disciple. But if you do the above, be forewarned. This is a 'dangerous' commentary because it reminds us from beginning to end that to be a Christian requires being like Jesus."

—**Charles Dunahoo**, Chairman of the Board, Westminster Theological Seminary

"Mention the call to be more like Christ, and questions instantly abound. All serious believers instinctively think the task is impossible, and many evangelicals wonder whether it is even something that we're supposed to do. Yet at the same time, we also sense that somehow the imitation of Christ is part and parcel of what it means to be a faithful Christian. How do we handle these questions, these competing attitudes? Even more important, how do we go about a task as enormous as being like Christ? In this wonderful little book, Jimmy Agan unpacks these questions and others like them through a careful, patient reading of Luke's gospel. He clearly shows us in what ways Jesus is unique as the Divine Son—and thus *not* a pattern for us to imitate. And the author tells us in what ways Jesus is fully human—and thus our perfect example of human life as God meant it to be. Agan's pastoral wisdom, sympathy for the struggles we face as Christians, and conversational writing style bring the fruit of his scholarship on Luke to a level that any serious Christian can understand. I recommend this book most highly!"

—**Donald Fairbairn**, Robert E. Cooley Professor of Early Christianity, Gordon-Conwell Theological Seminary

"This book is a gift to me as a pastor, father, husband, professor, communitarian, and friend! Jimmy's work is a manual for training Christians to imitate Christ with a gospel-centered focus and a spiritually joyful heart. No one can read this book and fail to conclude that Christ's sacrifice is the motivation for following him and that the Father's love is the power to do it. With the gospel so clearly unveiled in every chapter, one who follows this guide will inevitably conclude that because the yoke belongs to Jesus, it is easy and his burden is light."

—**George W. Robertson**, Senior Pastor, First Presbyterian Church (PCA), Augusta, Georgia

"Some books are eloquent, some are passionate, and some are wise. This book is all three. It makes a convincing case for deep reflection on Jesus' example, leading to sustained effort to be like him. Agan flags the dangers of the imitation-of-Christ project. But he maps us past the risks, with Scripture as GPS and conformity to Christ as destination. Engrossing and stirring, this is the finest succinct statement on the subject in recent times."

—**Robert W. Yarbrough**, Professor of New Testament, Covenant Theological Seminary

# *The* Imitation *of* Christ *in the* Gospel *of* Luke

# *The* Imitation *of* Christ *in the* Gospel *of* Luke

## Growing in Christlike Love for God and Neighbor

C.D. "JIMMY" AGAN III

P U B L I S H I N G
P.O. BOX 817 • PHILLIPSBURG • NEW JERSEY 08865-0817

Italics within Scripture quotations indicate emphasis added.

ISBN: 978-1-59638-216-9 (pbk)
ISBN: 978-1-59638-647-1 (ePub)
ISBN: 978-1-59638-648-8 (Mobi)

Printed in the United States of America

**Library of Congress Cataloging-in-Publication Data**

Agan, Jimmy.
The imitation of Christ in the gospel of Luke : growing in Christlike love for God and neighbor / C.D. Jimmy Agan III.
pages cm
Includes bibliographical references and index.
ISBN 978-1-59638-216-9 (pbk.)
1. Bible. Luke--Criticism, interpretation, etc. 2. Jesus Christ--Example. 3. Imitation--Religious aspects. I. Title.
BS2595.52.A33 2014
226.4'06--dc23

2013033942

For Tricia
Beloved bride, faithful friend, and true model of Christlike hospitality

# Contents

# PREFACE

CHRISTIANS INTUITIVELY UNDERSTAND that their lives should reflect the character and conduct of Jesus. This makes sense, not only because we believe Jesus lived a life of perfect obedience and love, but because God is at work conforming us "to the image of his Son" (Rom. 8:29). So if you ask any Christian—and perhaps many non-Christians—to summarize their vision for spiritual maturity, they will likely include something along these lines:

"I want to reflect the image of Christ in my daily life."
"I want to grow in likeness to Christ."
"I want to be more like Jesus."

Most people who have such goals know that Jesus is more than an example, and that the Gospels of Matthew, Mark, Luke, and John are not merely collections of "be like Jesus" stories. Still, we have a deep longing to be "imitators . . . of Christ" (1 Cor. 11:1) and to base our imitation on biblical accounts of his life. And so we turn to the Gospels, believing that as we read we can identify patterns in Jesus' life that we should mirror in our own.

If the previous paragraph describes you at all, I have good news—and bad. The good news is that this book aims to help you grow as an imitator of Christ by enabling you to see and respond to Jesus' example as it is presented in Luke's Gospel. The bad news is that this is not as simple as it might seem, for two reasons. First, the Gospels themselves don't give us much explicit instruction on how to pattern our lives after Jesus' example. Jesus' words in John 13:14–15 illustrate the point: "If I then, your Lord and Teacher, have washed your feet, you also ought to wash one another's feet. For I have given you an example, that you also should do just as I have done to you." Clearly, Jesus has provided an example to be imitated. But who should imitate him—the apostles? Later church leaders? All Christians? And how should they imitate him—by literally washing one another's feet? Or by loving and serving one another in ways that are symbolized by this action? While we can look to the broader context of John's Gospel for clues, the text never gives definitive answers to these questions. Nor does it offer guidelines for separating those aspects of Jesus' life that are unique to his role as "Lord and Teacher" from those that are to be imitated. Since the Gospels don't spell out such things for us, careful reflection is required if we are to grasp what they have to teach us about imitating Christ.

Second, the kind of careful reflection required for reading the Gospels as imitators of Christ is rarely encouraged by our churches. For reasons discussed in chapter 1, this is especially true in traditions that maintain the theological commitments of the Protestant Reformation. In such circles, the topic of the imitation of Christ is often neglected, as though the message of the Gospels were, "Jesus is Savior—so there's no example to see here!" (Such neglect probably explains why one student, when he learned that I was working on a book on this topic, asked, "Are you allowed to do that?") So, while Reformation commitments have inspired generations of scholars and pastors to think carefully about interpreting and applying Scripture, this care has not always extended to the matter of reading the Gospels in order to grow in likeness to Christ. As a result, the door is opened to abuse, as believers turn to resources that emphasize being like Jesus, but lack careful grounding in Scripture. Well-known examples include Charles Sheldon's best-selling book *In His Steps* and the WWJD movement it inspired; both are based on a partial picture of Christ's person and work, and encourage speculation about what Jesus *would* do rather than thoughtful reflection on what Jesus *did* do.

Ultimately, then, this book hopes to guard against *abuse* of the imitation of Christ by correcting the *neglect* of the imitation of Christ. In order to allow for more in-depth study, I have chosen to focus on the Gospel according to Luke. The main reason for this choice is familiarity, as I have been studying, teaching, and preaching from Luke's Gospel for more than fifteen years. This means that some readers will be disappointed because their favorite Gospel account from Matthew, Mark, or John is not discussed. Others will be disappointed because I have not used language associated with Paul's letters (e.g., "conformity with Christ"), or have not discussed the imitation of Christ as it relates to the categories of systematic theology (e.g., "union with Christ"). These omissions result from my desire to focus on Luke, not from any hostility toward other biblical writers, terms, or doctrines. Still, the hope is that the principles applied here to Luke's Gospel could be applied to other Gospels. To the extent that the conclusions I reach reflect Luke's intended meaning, they will certainly be compatible with the teaching of Scripture as a whole.

But what if the opening paragraph of this preface *doesn't* describe you? What if you don't want to be like Jesus? Perhaps this book can still be of help to you. If you aren't convinced that the imitation of Christ should be a central feature of the Christian life, I hope the discussion in chapters 1 and 2 will increase your appreciation for this biblical theme. If imitating Christ sounds to you like an impossible or impractical ideal—or worse, like a burden that would threaten to crush your soul—you may want to turn directly to chapters 13 and 14 for a reminder of the resources God has provided to make growth in Christlikeness possible. And if you are not a Christian, or if you are a Christian whose zeal for spiritual growth has grown cold over time, I hope that this book will help you to see Jesus in all his splendor, so that an overwhelming desire to belong to him, to trust in him, and even to imitate him is created in you. As 1 John 3:2 suggests, we need to see Jesus if we want to be like him. May this book help us to do both.

# Acknowledgments

WITHOUT THE HELP and encouragement of many others, the writing of this book would have been impossible. In particular, I would like to express my gratitude to the following people.

- The staff of P&R Publishing, especially John Hughes, Mary Ruth Murdoch, and Barbara Lerch, whose expertise—and patience—were invaluable.
- Those who assisted with bibliographical research: Dan Herron and Aaron White, and Covenant Seminary librarians Jim Pakala and Steve Jamieson.
- Those who read the manuscript and offered helpful feedback: Michael Davis, Will Esler, and Ed and Jenny Savage.
- Rick Matt and Dr. Chris Morgan, whose editorial help strengthened the manuscript in countless ways.
- Dr. Robert Peterson, who has offered not only expertise but encouragement at every step of the way.
- Prof. I. Howard Marshall, of the University of Aberdeen, and Dr. David Jones, of Covenant Seminary, who originally stimulated my interest in the topic.
- Those whose ongoing encouragement enabled me to persevere: Donnagail Carr, Charlie and Rae Gibson, Dr. Mike Honeycutt, Peter Karutz, Geoff Rigabar, and above all my family—Tricia, Sarah Elizabeth, Caroline, Patrick, and Abby.

# I

# Why You Should *Not* Read This Book: Arguments against the Imitation of Christ

IS IT FAIR to have a strike against you before you ever pick up a bat? In many softball leagues, the answer is, "Yes!" To avoid long innings and even longer games, many slow-pitch softball leagues adopt a rule intended to speed up play: the batter begins with a strike against him. But if that seems unfair, imagine a league in which players come to the plate with *three* strikes against them—they would be out before they even step into the batter's box!

This is the situation for the imitation of Christ. Many Christians understand intuitively that growing in likeness to Jesus is an essential component of Christian discipleship, and they naturally turn to the Gospels for instruction on how to be like Jesus. Yet over the centuries, some serious objections have been raised against this very notion. As a result, many biblical scholars, theologians, and pastors treat the topic as though it were "out" before the game began. This is true among many Protestants, and especially among those who would consider themselves Reformed (that is, committed to the doctrinal distinctives of Protestant Reformation leaders like Martin Luther, John Calvin, and their theological heirs). Author E. J. Tinsley has summarized this tension well:

> The idea of the imitation of Christ has an ambivalent status in the history of Christian spirituality. On the one hand it has been taken to be the classical and normative way of characterizing the Christian spiritual life. . . . On the other hand there are those, chiefly of the Reformed traditions, who have felt that the idea of the imitation of Christ matches ill with the Christian doctrine of grace.[1]

Our aim in this book is to learn what Luke's Gospel has to teach us about imitating Christ. But before our study can proceed, we need to understand the nature of the objections to the imitation of Christ—what they are, why they have arisen, and what they teach us about errors we must take care to avoid.

In chapter 2, we will see that there are sound biblical and theological responses to the objections against the imitation of Christ, so that my writing, and your reading, of this book is not an exercise in futility. But for now, even though it will involve hearing only one side of the issue, we want to feel the weight of the objections—objections that make some people fear that the imitation of Christ has three strikes against it before the first pitch is thrown.

## The Evangelical Argument: Imitation Diminishes Christ's Person and Work

Who is Jesus? And what did he accomplish, especially by his *death*? In the late 1800s and early 1900s, many biblical scholars

1. E. J. Tinsley, "Imitation of Christ," in *A Dictionary of Christian Spirituality*, ed. Gordon S. Wakefield (London: SCM Press, 1988), 208. Tinsley is best known for his book *The Imitation of God in Christ: An Essay on the Biblical Basis of Christian Spirituality* (London: SCM Press, 1960).

and theologians (who were later known as "liberals" or "modernists") sought to answer these questions in terms of human reason, and without reference to anything purported to be supernatural. The implications for the first of our questions—Who is Jesus?—were staggering: all that remained was a "Jesus" who was little more than an enlightened teacher and an example of love. His death saved not by satisfying God's justice or by absorbing the penalty sin deserved, but through its moral impact on the human heart. As Douglas Macintosh, a nineteenth-century proponent of liberalism, put it: "Christianity is the religion of deliverance from unchristlikeness to a Christlike morality, through a Christlike attitude towards a Christlike superhuman reality."[2] In other words, Jesus saves by giving us an example to imitate.

Contrast McIntosh's summary of Christianity with that of J. Gresham Machen, an outspoken opponent of liberalism:

> Liberalism regards [Jesus] as an Example and Guide; Christianity, as a Saviour: liberalism makes Him an example for faith; Christianity, the object of faith.
>
> He is our Saviour, not because He has inspired us to live the same kind of life that He lived, but because He took upon Himself the dreadful guilt of our sins and bore it instead of us on the cross.[3]

Given these starkly opposing visions, it is not difficult to see why "evangelicals" (as those opposed to liberalism have come to be known) are suspicious of the imitation of Christ—a concept often associated with the denial of biblical truth about Jesus and his saving work. Nuanced reminders that Jesus' example does have a proper place in the Christian life can be hard to hear on the

2. As cited in B. B. Warfield, *Christology and Criticism* (New York: Oxford University Press, 1929), 411.

3. J. Gresham Machen, *Christianity and Liberalism* (Grand Rapids: Eerdmans, 1946), 96, 117.

theological battlefield; as a result, the imitation of Christ has become a casualty of war. Perhaps its wounds are not fatal, but in evangelical circles, imitation will forever walk with a limp.

## The Augustinian Argument: Imitation Denies Human Need of Divine Grace

The next two strikes against the imitation of Christ are associated with key moments in church history. The first occurred in the late 300s A.D., when a teacher named Pelagius, troubled by the moral laxity of Christians in Rome, began to emphasize the ability of believers to make real progress in holiness. To defend his notion of human ability, Pelagius denied that human beings were corrupt or "fallen" as a result of Adam's sin. Here Pelagius appealed to the concept of imitation: we sin not because we are born corrupt, but because we are following bad examples—whether the bad example of Adam, or the bad example of others around us. As Pelagius's teaching spread, many were concerned that it left no place for the grace of God. If we are not corrupted by sin, and are capable of righteous living, why would we need God's grace to redeem us or to enable us to grow in holiness? Pelagius responded with a new, "external" interpretation of grace. Rather than God's transforming grace at work *in* us, he argued, we need to take advantage of the grace God has already given *to* us: capacity to do good, Christ's sacrifice to pardon us when we sin, and Christ's example to replace the bad examples we follow.

It was left to Augustine, a North African bishop, to demonstrate the radical flaws in such teaching. Arguing that human beings are in fact fallen and in need of something more than the external grace Pelagius championed, Augustine returned again and again to Romans 5:12–21. Pelagius insisted that Paul had imitation in mind here: "all sinned" (Rom. 5:12) by imitating the sin of Adam. Augustine argued on several grounds that this could not be Paul's meaning. Most importantly, the Adam/Christ parallel in Romans 5 teaches that we become righteous not by imitating Christ, but by receiving "the free gift of righteousness" through Christ's work on our behalf (Rom. 5:17). We cannot be made righteous by following Christ's good example, because Adam's sin is not merely a bad example. Rather, its guilt and power have been passed on to every one of his race. Only by God's grace, understood not as an external gift but as a radical transformation of the sinful human heart, can we become part of a new race, that of Christ the Redeemer.

Augustine's arguments were so compelling that even today the very notion of the imitation of Christ often comes under immediate suspicion. For instance, we hear echoes of Augustine when British theologian Alister McGrath remarks that "[s]anctification . . . is about becoming Christlike, not by imitating Christ but by being changed by the grace of God. . . . Imitation brings in its wake a whole range of ideas and attitudes that are profoundly hostile to the gospel of grace."[4] And, as we saw earlier, E. J. Tinsley attributes nervousness about imitation, especially among "the Reformed traditions," to fear that it "conceals a moral endeavour of a *Pelagian* kind."[5] And so the second strike is called—for to speak too highly of the imitation of Christ is to sound like one of the church's earliest and most notorious heretics.

## The Reformation Argument: Imitation Exalts Christ as Example over Christ as Gift

To understand why Tinsley mentions the Reformed tradition as particularly suspicious of the imitation of Christ, we must turn to a second key moment in church history. In the sixteenth century, a Roman Catholic monk named Martin Luther began to realize that the teaching and practice of his church were in dire need of reform according to Scripture. Luther's biblical insights

4. Alister McGrath, "In What Way Can Jesus Be a Moral Example for Christians?," *Journal of the Evangelical Theological Society* 34, 3 (September 1991): 297.

5. Tinsley, "Imitation of Christ," 208, emphasis added.

would ultimately lead to the Protestant Reformation—and to a strong condemnation of imitation as it was practiced at the time.

Three emphases related to the imitation of Christ featured prominently in sixteenth-century Catholic thought and life. First, many church leaders appealed to Christ's example when calling Christians to take up vows of celibacy or poverty as priests, monks, or nuns. Luther, by contrast, stressed the notion that all of life is to be lived to the glory of God, so that one need not forsake ordinary duties in order to follow Christ.

Second, for many, imitation had come to mean outward conformity to some action of Jesus, the apostles, or a saint. For instance, church leaders would often defend the custom of fasting during Lent by noting that Jesus had fasted for forty days in the wilderness. Luther was quick to point out that what mattered was not such external correspondence, but the formation of one's character and motives. And while he had deep respect for holy men and women of old, Luther could not abide the thought of yielding to them an authority that belongs only to Christ.

Third, and most complex, was an introspective, mystical approach to imitating Christ. Here the imitator sought to follow the pattern of Jesus' death and resurrection, first going through affliction and spiritual "death" in order to cultivate humility, and then giving himself over to God in hopes of "rebirth." In keeping with sixteenth-century doctrine, this approach assumed the ability of sinners to prepare themselves for salvation ("rebirth"). As Luther, like Augustine, came to see that only a heart supernaturally transformed by God's grace could desire holiness, he rejected this model of "preparation-through-imitation" as Pelagian. As popular as it was, the mystical approach to imitation would have to be rejected, since it denied the biblical truth of salvation by grace alone, through faith alone.[6]

6. For more detail, see Alister E. McGrath, *Luther's Theology of the Cross: Martin Luther's Theological Breakthrough* (Oxford and New York: Basil Blackwell, 1985).

Two representative quotes underscore Luther's desire to correct a misguided emphasis on the imitation of Christ. In his 1535 lectures on Galatians, Luther insists that Christ "must be grasped by faith as a gift, not as an example," for "imitation of the example of Christ does not make us righteous in the sight of God." He concludes that the "Christ who blesses and redeems is vastly different from Christ the example." Elsewhere he warns that to speak of Christ only as example is to "make of him a severe and angry judge, a fearful and horrible tyrant, full of wrath against poor sinners, and bent on condemning them."[7] To be sure, Luther had much more to say on the topic of imitating Christ, and not all of his comments were as negative as these. Yet the Protestant and Reformed tradition has tended to remember Luther as one who offers us a choice: either Christ is gift and merciful Savior, or—strike three—example and tyrannical judge.

## The Heart's Cry: Imitation Demands the Impossible

Could you live like Jesus? Could you live like him for a year? The title of a *USA Today* online article asked this very question, prompting hundreds of responses. One reader replied, "I don't think ANY of us could live like Jesus for one day." Another agreed: "No man can live like Jesus."[8] These quotes crystallize one final objection to the imitation of Christ, which we may summarize as follows: "Being like Jesus sounds great. But it's impossible. I can't do it."

Sometimes this objection arises from a keen sense of human sinfulness in general: any suggestion that morally bankrupt

7. References are to Martin Luther, "Lectures on Galatians, 1535," in *Luther's Works*, American Edition, 55 vols., ed. Jaroslav Pelikan and Helmut T. Lehmann (Philadelphia: Muhlenberg and Fortress and St. Louis: Concordia, 1955–86), 26:246–47; and Martin Luther, *The Table Talk of Martin Luther*, ed. Thomas S. Kepler (Grand Rapids: Baker, 1952), 115.

8. Charles Honey, "Could you live like Jesus for a year? This pastor tried," USAToday.com, http://www.usatoday.com/news/religion/2009-01-01-jesus-year_N.htm (accessed January 28, 2011).

sinners could imitate Christ sounds like arrogance. "We're sinners," we might say, "so any attempt to be like Jesus will only reveal the impossibility of the task." But sometimes this objection arises from a sense of hopelessness based on personal experience with sin. The heart that is broken from bearing the weight of its own corruption can feel the call to imitate Christ not as an invitation to spiritual growth, but as mockery: "Me? Like Jesus? What is this, some kind of cruel joke?" Even as I write these words, I wrestle with such thoughts. I know my own failings, my own history of sinning, my own tendency to abandon holiness at the first sign of serious temptation. And so I understand completely when students, church members, family, or friends wince as if in pain when I suggest to them that the imitation of Christ really should have a prominent place in our lives. "Maybe in some of our lives. But never in mine."

## Conclusion

No study of the imitation of Christ can afford to ignore the cumulative effect of the objections we have surveyed. Our heritage as evangelicals, shaped by battles against theological liberalism, causes us to shrink back from any teaching that might undermine biblical teaching about Christ and his saving death. Our heritage as Protestants, echoing with the voices of leaders like Augustine and Luther, leads us to suspect that imitation is a cover for works-righteousness, a denial of the grace of God as our only hope for salvation. And, most painfully, when anyone suggests that we should imitate Christ, our own hearts hear the mocking voices of all of our failures, past, present, and future. "He's already out! Three strikes against him before he even stepped to the plate," some voices cry. Yet none of the objections raised so far represents the full scope of biblical truth on the matter. And so, in chapter 2 we will hear Scripture reply, "But who said we were playing by those rules?"

# 2

# Why You *Should* Read This Book: Arguments for the Imitation of Christ

"GIVE ME ONE GOOD REASON . . ." Each of us has used this phrase, in contexts ranging from the political ("Give me one good reason to vote your way!") to the personal ("Give me one good reason to trust you again!") or even the parental ("Can you give me one good reason to let you dye your hair blue?"). These five words signal that we're having a hard time accepting what we're hearing. They also suggest that, even though we aren't closed-minded, we doubt whether there is any reason strong enough to change our minds. In light of the weighty objections raised in chapter 1, it would be fair for readers of this book to adopt a "one good reason" attitude: is there even *one* good reason for risking our commitment to Jesus the Savior by giving time and attention to Jesus the Example?

In this chapter, I hope to give you not one but *four* good reasons for taking seriously an appropriate, biblical understanding of imitating Christ. Though the objections of chapter 1 will always need to stand as warnings, they should not make us so cautious that we neglect the clear testimony of Scripture. It is with that testimony that this chapter will open, as we survey major New Testament texts that call for the imitation of Christ. If I want to help you change your mind, I need to give *good* reasons—and those that flow from careful attention to Scripture are the best I could hope to give.

## The Imitation of Christ: A Survey of New Testament Teaching

What follows is an overview of the most important New Testament texts related to the imitation of Christ. To keep our study at a reasonable length, we are not able to include every relevant text, or to give detailed treatment of any single text. However, even this brief survey will demonstrate the important role that the imitation of Christ plays in the New Testament.[1]

### *Imitate Me, as I Imitate Christ*

Perhaps the most obvious starting point for our survey is 1 Corinthians 11:1, where Paul urges readers, "Be imitators of me, as I am of Christ." Rather than an arrogant assertion of Paul's ego or a vague spiritual platitude, this verse represents Paul's hope that his spiritual children will grow up to bear the family likeness (see 1 Cor. 4:14–16). As the context indicates, Christ models two patterns that govern the proper exercise of Christian freedom in a non-Christian culture: concern to do "all to the glory of God" (1 Cor. 10:31), and a commitment to seeking the "advantage . . . of many, that they may be saved" (1 Cor. 10:33). If

1. In our survey, the term *imitation* is often used as shorthand for the imitation of Christ, though there are a few New Testament texts that call for the imitation of God, and several that call for the imitation of human figures.

these Christlike priorities had featured more prominently in the life of the church, perhaps many of the problems Paul addresses in 1 Corinthians could have been prevented.

### *The Grace of Christ and the Grace of Giving*

Paul points the Corinthians to Christ's example again as he calls them to contribute to an offering for needy Christians in Jerusalem: "For you know the grace of our Lord Jesus Christ, that though he was rich, yet for your sake he became poor, so that you by his poverty might become rich" (2 Cor. 8:9). Paul's appeal is asymmetrical; while Christ's grace toward us *accomplished* our redemption from spiritual poverty, our imitation of his example is a *response* to his redeeming work. It also employs a "though-not-but" pattern: *though* Christ possessed the riches of heavenly glory, he did *not* insist on keeping them for himself, *but* instead impoverished himself so that others could share in his wealth.[2] These two features consistently characterize biblical teaching on the imitation of Christ.

### *Bride and Groom, Church and Christ*

In Ephesians 5:25, Paul instructs husbands to love their wives "as Christ loved the church and gave himself up for her." The Christlike husband delights to help his wife flourish spiritually, as Christ has "sanctif[ied]" his bride so that she is "without blemish" (Eph. 5:26–27). Such a husband also "nourishes and cherishes" his wife, even at great cost to himself (Eph. 5:29). While marriage involves a specific application of the principle, Ephesians 5:2 ("walk in love, as Christ loved us and gave himself up for us") makes it clear that Christ's love is the pattern for relationships among all Christians.[3]

2. This terminology is from Michael J. Gorman, *Cruciformity: Paul's Narrative Spirituality of the Cross* (Grand Rapids and Cambridge: Eerdmans, 2001).

3. See also Rom. 15:1–3, 7; Eph. 4:32–5:1; and Col. 3:13.

### *The Mind of Christ, the Servant-Lord*

From Paul's letters, the final text to be mentioned in our survey is the *Carmen Christi* or "Christ hymn" of Philippians 2:5–11, which calls Christians to imitate the humble mindset seen in Christ. In Philippians 2:1–4, Paul exhorts the Philippian church to like-mindedness, mutual love, humility, and concern for the interests of others. He then summarizes the life of Christ through four key events: he "made himself nothing" (Phil. 2:7 NIV); he "humbled himself" through incarnation and crucifixion (Phil. 2:7–8); God "highly exalted him" (Phil. 2:9); God "bestowed on him the name that is above every name" (Phil. 2:9). Linking Paul's exhortations to the story of Christ is Philippians 2:5, which the NIV translates, "Your attitude should be the same as that of Christ Jesus."[4]

Three features of this text are of special interest for our study. First, the "though-not-but" rhythm characteristic of imitation texts is prominent here: *though* he possessed all the privileges of heavenly glory, Jesus did *not* selfishly cling to them, *but* instead lowered himself, in his incarnation, to the depths of humiliation. Second, while the text clearly portrays Christ as more than a mere human example, it also presents him as the model for Christian life. This is confirmed by the parallels between what we are called to do (e.g., "in humility count others more significant than yourselves," Phil. 2:3) and what he has done (e.g., "he humbled himself," Phil. 2:8). Third, while Christ's exaltation to divine glory (Phil. 2:9–11) cannot be imitated, this theme supports the call to Christlikeness by assuring us that God does ultimately bless a life of self-sacrificial humility. There is only one Servant-Lord, but the path of humility and service which he followed is intended for all who trust in him.

4. The ESV translation ("Have this mind among yourselves, which is yours in Christ Jesus") places more emphasis on union with Christ than on the imitation of Christ.

### *Servanthood That Outweighs the World*

The humility of the Servant-Lord is also emphasized in the ransom saying, in which Jesus himself calls for the imitation of his example:

> You know that those who are considered rulers of the Gentiles lord it over them, and their great ones exercise authority over them. But it shall not be so among you. But whoever would be great among you must be your servant, and whoever would be first among you must be slave of all. For even the Son of Man came not to be served but to serve, and to give his life as a ransom for many. (Mark 10:42–45; see also Matt. 20:25–28)

*Though* he is the Son of Man (the glorious heavenly figure of Dan. 7:13–14, who is "served" by all nations), Jesus did *not* come to be served, *but* to serve. This pattern culminates in his death, which ransoms his followers from sin and judgment—and which lends such force to his example that it outweighs the patterns of leadership which pervade our world. As the suffering Son of Man, Jesus is Lord, Savior, and example, with neither reality undermining the others.[5]

### *Taking Up a Cross to Follow Jesus*

In Mark 8:34 and its parallels (Matt. 16:24; Luke 9:23), Jesus issues a challenge that is central to any discussion of imitation: "If anyone would come after me, let him deny himself and take up his cross and follow me." Given that this verse follows Jesus' prediction of his own death and resurrection (Mark 8:31), it is clear that we as disciples must, like him, willingly endure rejection, humiliation, and suffering in the present, trusting God to restore our honor in the future. The concepts of self-denial and

5. A similar text, found at Luke 22:24–27, will be discussed in detail in chapter 9.

cross-bearing will be discussed in detail in chapters 9 and 10 below. For now, however, we draw two conclusions: first, even during Jesus' lifetime the call to bear the cross would have been a powerful summons for disciples to shape their lives according to the pattern of the Master's; second, this call is even more powerful now that we have seen the full extent of Jesus' own cross-bearing!

### *Footwashing as a Symbol of Self-Sacrificial Love*

According to John 13:14–15, during the Last Supper Jesus washes the feet of his disciples, returns to his place at the table, and issues a charge: "If I then, your Lord and Teacher, have washed your feet, you also ought to wash one another's feet. For I have given you an example, that you also should do just as I have done to you." Similarities with John 13:34 confirm that we are not to imitate the act of footwashing itself, but the self-sacrificial love it symbolizes: "A new commandment I give to you, that you love one another: just as I have loved you, you also are to love one another." As Jesus loved us "to the end" (John 13:1) by setting aside privilege and status to serve us from the despised place of the cross, so we are to love one another.

### *Jesus as the Example of Faith and Endurance*

The readers of Hebrews faced a choice: endure increasing Roman hostility by continuing to confess Christ, or escape persecution by denying Christ. It is against this background that we are to read Hebrews 12:1–3:

> Let us run with endurance the race that is set before us, looking to Jesus, the founder and perfecter of our faith, who for the joy that was set before him endured the cross, despising the shame, and is seated at the right hand of the

> throne of God. Consider him who endured from sinners such hostility against himself, so that you may not grow weary or fainthearted.

In the endurance of shame, suffering, and persecution, it is Jesus who is our model. The description of Jesus as the "founder and perfecter of our faith" also suggests (among other depths of meaning) that Jesus is a model of faith. By trusting God's promises of coming "joy" while on the cross, Jesus has embodied faith more completely than any human being before or since. As the enthroned Messiah, seated at God's "right hand," Jesus is more than a model; but when the author of Hebrews needs to move his readers to faith and endurance in the face of suffering, Jesus' example is a key part of his appeal.

### *In the Steps of the Suffering Savior*

We close our survey with 1 Peter 2:21–23, which calls believers to Christlike endurance of undeserved hostility:

> For to this you have been called, because Christ also suffered for you, leaving you an example, so that you might follow in his steps. He committed no sin, neither was deceit found in his mouth. When he was reviled, he did not revile in return; when he suffered, he did not threaten, but continued entrusting himself to him who judges justly.

As in Hebrews, here Jesus is an example of patient endurance and trust in God. Two themes are noteworthy. First, Peter sees no tension between Jesus' unique, sin-bearing work and our calling to imitate him; the Savior who suffered "for us" is also our example. Second, Peter mentions Jesus' sinlessness not to discourage us, but to provide us with even more powerful motivation: if Jesus refrained from sin even as he endured the cross in our place, then we who face lesser trials should be ready to follow "in his steps."[6]

## Four Arguments in Favor of Studying the Imitation of Christ

In light of our survey of New Testament teaching, and in response to the objections of chapter 1, we may now summarize four reasons that Christians should devote significant attention to the imitation of Christ. More reasons could certainly be added, but these strike me as the most significant.

### *The Biblical Argument: Imitation Is an Important Part of New Testament Teaching*

We begin with this simple fact: the New Testament abounds with exhortations to follow Christ's example. These exhortations are, of course, presented within a broader understanding of who Christ is and what he has done for us; in chapters 3 and 13, we will see how Luke's Gospel provides such a framework for the imitation of Christ. For now, however, we want to hear the clear testimony of the Scriptures: *deep reflection on Jesus' example, leading to sustained effort to be like him, is a central feature of the Christian life*. Not only is this conviction expressed in the New Testament, it appears at key moments: just after a prediction of Jesus' death; in the Upper Room, just before his arrest and crucifixion; when the church needs instruction in love, generosity, and humility; when believers need courage to face persecution. While the imitation of Christ is not the central theme of the New Testament, it would be unwise to neglect a theme that plays such a pivotal role in God's Word.

6. Peter's original audience included domestic slaves (1 Peter 2:18) and others facing persecution for Christ's sake; therefore, it is wrong to conclude that this text obligates people to *voluntarily* remain in abusive relationships or dangerous situations.

### *The Historical Argument: Imitation Has an Important Place in Reformed Heritage*

Protestant and Reformed believers sometimes fear that an emphasis on the imitation of Christ is at odds with their spiritual heritage. However, that heritage includes leaders who knew how to affirm strongly the *proper use* of imitation, even while condemning its *abuses*. J. Gresham Machen, for instance, often spoke of liberalism and Christianity as two different religions, one emphasizing Christ as our example and the other emphasizing Christ as our Savior. Yet he could also affirm that "[t]he imitation of Jesus has a fundamental place in Christian life; it is perfectly correct to represent Him as our supreme and only perfect example."[7]

But what of our Reformation-era forebears? While we cited some of Luther's criticisms in chapter 1, the point he makes most frequently about imitation is that it goes hand in hand with faith in Christ's saving work. Thus he writes, "For when we have put on Christ, the garment of our righteousness and salvation, then we also put on Christ, the garment of imitation."[8] Similarly, offering instruction on how to read the Gospels, Luther says, "Now when you have Christ as the foundation and chief blessing of your salvation, then the other part follows: that you take him as your example."[9] John Calvin gave the imitation of Christ an even more prominent role, opening his most systematic discussion of the Christian life with this assertion: "Christ, through whom we return into favor with God, has been set before us as

7. J. Gresham Machen, *Christianity and Liberalism* (1923; repr. Grand Rapids, Eerdmans, 1946), 93.

8. Martin Luther, "Lectures on Galatians, 1535," in *Luther's Works*, American Edition, 55 vols., ed. Jaroslav Pelikan and Helmut T. Lehmann (Philadelphia: Muhlenberg and Fortress/St. Louis: Concordia, 1955–86), 26:353.

9. Martin Luther, "A Brief Instruction on What to Look for and Expect in the Gospels," in *Luther's Works*, American Edition, 55 vols., ed. Jaroslav Pelikan and Helmut T. Lehmann (Philadelphia: Muhlenberg and Fortress and St. Louis: Concordia, 1955–86), 35:120.

an example, whose pattern we ought to express in our life."[10] Elsewhere Calvin says, more simply, "to imitate Christ . . . is the rule of life."[11]

As these few, but representative, citations attest, many Protestant and Reformed leaders have recognized that when it comes to the imitation of Christ, *abuse does not negate proper use*. If a little boy uses his father's hammer to destroy a priceless piece of furniture, the solution is not to ban hammers from the home, but to teach the little boy how to use the hammer properly, how he endangers himself and others if he misuses it, and which jobs require a different tool. It is wise to be able to recognize and avoid abuses of the imitation of Christ; it is equally wise to commit ourselves to putting this theme to its proper, biblical use. When Protestant and Reformed believers agree with such reasoning, we are not departing from our heritage, but maintaining it.[12]

### *The Pastoral Argument: Imitation Promotes Love and Combats Despair*

As one who is a pastor and a teacher of pastors, I see several benefits for individual Christians, families, and churches in a renewed focus on following Christ's example. First, careful attention to this theme will increase in us a *Christlike love for those who are not Christians*. As we focus on Christ's example

10. John Calvin, *Institutes of the Christian Religion*, 2 vols., ed. John T. McNeill, The Library of Christian Classics, vol. 20 (Louisville, London, and Leiden: Westminster John Knox, 1960), 3.6.3. For Calvin's condemnation of the abuses of imitation, see *Institutes*, 4.12.20; 4.19.7; 4.19.29.

11. John Calvin, *Calvin's New Testament Commentaries*, 12 vols., ed. David W. Torrance and Thomas F. Torrance (repr.; Grand Rapids: Eerdmans, 1989), 11:246 (commenting on Phil. 2:5).

12. Unfortunately, some contemporary writers cite the objections of Luther and Calvin to the imitation of Christ without any indication that the Reformers also had positive things to say about the topic. See Michael Horton, *The Christian Faith: A Systematic Theology for Pilgrims on the Way* (Grand Rapids: Zondervan, 2011), esp. chapter 18, "Union with Christ"; and F. Scott Spencer, "Imitation of Jesus," in *Dictionary of Scripture and Ethics*, ed. Joel B. Green (Grand Rapids: Baker, 2011).

of self-sacrificial love for sinners, and his desire "to seek and to save the lost" (Luke 19:10), we will see similar fruit in our lives.

Second, careful study of the imitation of Christ will promote *Christlike love among believers and within congregations*. As our earlier survey showed, Christians are to love one another, please one another, and forgive one another—all as Christ has done for us, and all in the context of daily concerns such as marriage, care for those experiencing financial need, and disagreements among believers. Careful attention to the example of Christ will therefore call us to repentance, humility, and love in precisely those areas where relationships are most likely to fracture.

Finally, I am convinced that careful study of the imitation of Christ will give us *encouragement when we despair of progress toward spiritual maturity*. Calvin recognizes this in his comment on Hebrews 12:3: "when we realize that we are the companions of the Son of God and that He who was so far above us was willing to come down to our condition to encourage us by His example . . . we gain new heart when otherwise we would melt away and dissolve into despair."[13] Careful study of this theme will always bring us face to face with a Savior who forgives sin, heals the brokenhearted, and sustains the weary by the power of his Spirit.

### The Doxological Argument: Imitation Enhances God's Praise

To speak of a "doxological" argument for studying the imitation of Christ is to say that such study will prompt praise (*doxa*) of God. This will happen in several ways:

- As we begin to demonstrate greater likeness to Christ, we will become *living testimonies to the triumph of divine grace*. Apart from Christ, our lives could never bear any

13. Calvin, *Calvin's New Testament Commentaries*, 12:189.

fruit; but because of his grace, our lives bear fruit that resembles the root from which they stem—Christ's work of redemption.

- Rightly understood, our efforts to be like Jesus will declare our *utmost delight in and allegiance to him*, showing that we value him more than comfort, status, prosperity, or even life itself.
- If we follow the New Testament's emphasis on Christ as our example, we will continually *exalt him as our only Savior*—for the two truths can never be separated.

Commenting on Philippians 2:8, Calvin captures the sense of wonder that should flow from serious reflection on imitating Christ: "[Christ's death is] assuredly such an example of humility as ought to absorb the attention of all men; it is impossible to explain it in words suitable to its greatness."[14]

## Conclusion

To give serious attention to the imitation of Christ is to honor the teaching of Scripture, to equip ourselves to distinguish the abuse of this biblical theme from its proper use, and to continue the heritage of Protestant and Reformed leaders who did likewise. When we seek to imitate Christ, we also pursue a path that by God's mercy will yield fruit for our growth, for others' good, and for the glory of the Triune God. With these goals in mind, we turn now to Luke's Gospel, as we let the unspeakable greatness of Christ and his example absorb our attention.

14. Ibid., 11:249.

# 3

# Getting Oriented, Part I: Jesus as Son of God and Second Adam in Luke

THE CEREMONY WAS OVER, and the guests had just been dismissed. As they left, the five-year-old flower girl tugged on my pant leg and posed her question: "Who died?" Thinking that she might be confused, I said, "Nobody died, sweetie. This was a wedding, not a funeral. It's a happy time." But she persisted. "No, you said somebody died. Who was it?" She was right. During the homily, based on Ephesians 5, I had spoken about Jesus, who loved his bride enough to die in her place, so that she might share in his joy. This little girl was not only attentive, she was wise. She knew that to benefit from what she had heard, she needed a clear answer to her question. Knowing that Jesus died makes no difference if you don't know who Jesus is.

As we begin our study of the imitation of Christ in Luke's Gospel, we are in a similar situation. Nothing we learn about being like Jesus will make any difference without a clear understanding of who he is. In this chapter, we will see that Luke answers this question in two parts: on the one hand, Jesus is the Son of God, the Messiah of Israel who has come for the salvation of the world; on the other, he is the second Adam, fully sharing in our humanity, yet living faithfully where we have failed. Key texts from the early portions of Luke will enable us to see how these truths run throughout the Gospel; then, based on what we have learned about who Jesus is, we will close our chapter by drawing five conclusions that are crucial for understanding and practicing the imitation of Christ.

## The Birth of the Son of God: Luke 1:26–38

The words of the angel Gabriel in Luke 1:30–33 make it clear that something incredible is about to happen: Mary will bear a child, Jesus, who "will be great and will be called the Son of the Most High. And the Lord God will give him the throne of his father David, and he will reign over the house of Jacob forever, and of his kingdom there will be no end." When Mary asks how it is possible for a virgin to bear a child, Gabriel's reply further reveals Jesus' identity: "The Holy Spirit will come upon you, and the power of the Most High will overshadow you; therefore the child to be born will be called holy—the Son of God" (Luke 1:35).

Son of God "Most High," Davidic king, everlasting ruler. It is in these exalted categories that Luke's Gospel introduces us to Jesus. To fully appreciate these descriptors, we need to recall three features of the Old Testament. First, we remember God's solemn promise that David's throne will "be established forever" (2 Sam. 7:16). Through David's line God will establish an everlasting kingdom characterized by peace (2 Sam. 7:10) and by the assurance of his own "steadfast love" (2 Sam. 7:15).

Second, while God is described as "Most High" throughout the Old Testament, this title is especially prominent in the book of Daniel, where it is associated with two themes: (1) God is sovereign over the kingdoms of the earth; (2) God will ultimately give his people an everlasting rule over all the earth.

Third, we remember Isaiah 9:6–7, which predicts the birth of a king so glorious that divine titles can properly be attributed to him. The italics in the following citation highlight language echoed by Gabriel in Luke 1:32–33:

> For to us *a child is born*, to us *a son* is given; and the government shall be upon his shoulder, and his name shall be called Wonderful Counselor, Mighty God, Everlasting Father, Prince of Peace. Of the increase of his government and of peace *there will be no end*, on *the throne of David* and over his *kingdom*, to establish it and to uphold it with justice and with righteousness from this time forth and forevermore.

According to Luke's Gospel, then, Jesus is the fulfillment of prophecies and promises on which the fate of God's people, and even of the whole earth, depends. More than that, he is the Son of God, entitled to share in the glory that belongs to God alone!

## Luke's Portrait of the Son of God

Given that Jesus' birth brings these Old Testament expectations to fulfillment, readers of Luke's Gospel are not surprised to discover that in many ways Jesus is unique, and cannot be imitated. A sampling of key themes makes this overwhelmingly clear:

1. *Jesus is the agent of ultimate blessing and judgment.* John the Baptist speaks of Jesus as one "mightier than I . . . the strap of whose sandals I am not worthy to untie. He will baptize you with the Holy Spirit and with fire" (Luke 3:16). Only Jesus can pour out God's ultimate blessing, the life-giving Spirit (Luke 24:49). And while others may

proclaim the coming day of judgment, Jesus alone is the judge who actually determines our eternal destiny (Luke 10:13–16; 11:29–32; 12:35–40; 13:22–30; 23:43).

2. *Jesus possesses unique, divine authority.* He can pronounce a person's sins forgiven (Luke 5:20; 7:48), command the wind and waves to obey him (Luke 8:24–25), and cast out demons and heal diseases "with authority" (Luke 4:31–41). While the apostles did perform miracles, it was Jesus who "gave them power and authority" to do so (Luke 9:1; 10:19). Likewise, they are commissioned not to pronounce but to "proclaim" the forgiveness of sins "in his name" (Luke 24:47).

3. *Jesus possesses unique, divine knowledge.* Unlike other biblical prophets who declare what God has revealed to them regarding future events, Jesus speaks of such events of his own accord. He speaks in detail of the destruction of Jerusalem and of the final judgment it foreshadows (Luke 21:5–32) and predicts that Peter will deny him three times before cockcrow (Luke 22:34). In addition, Jesus is able to discern the innermost thoughts of others, whether his critics (Luke 5:22; 6:8; 7:39–40) or his disciples (Luke 9:46).

4. *Jesus possesses powerful purity.* When Jesus touches a leper, he does not become unclean, as would any other person; rather, the leper is cleansed (Luke 5:12–15)! Similarly, instead of compromising his holiness, Jesus' contact with sinners brings about *their* repentance (Luke 7:34, 36–50; 15:1–2; 19:7).

5. *Jesus possesses divine glory.* On the Mount of Transfiguration, Jesus' dazzling brilliance recalls the heavenly splendor associated with angels and even with God himself (Luke 9:29; see Dan. 7:9; 10:6). Later, Jesus speaks openly

of sitting at God's right hand in glory (Luke 22:69). Most strikingly, when the resurrected Jesus ascends to heaven, his followers worship him (Luke 24:52). In this, Jesus is absolutely unique: no other person has ever been, or will ever be, both fully human and a proper object of worship.

If our study were to stop here, we might conclude that the thought of imitating Christ borders on blasphemy! Yet despite Luke's clear emphasis on Jesus' divinity and his unique status as the Son of God, there is an equally clear emphasis in Luke on Jesus' humanity—to which we now turn.

## A Truly Human Savior: Luke 3:21–22

According to Luke's Gospel, Jesus' uniqueness as the Son of God does not prevent him from sharing our humanity. In fact, Luke 3:21–4:13, where we read of Jesus' baptism, genealogy, and temptation in the wilderness, presents Jesus as one who is "truly human" in two senses: he really is a human being, completely sharing our human nature; and he is humanity as God intends it to be, remaining true to God's purpose where we have strayed.

Luke 3:21–22 recounts Jesus' baptism in a way that highlights both his uniqueness as Savior and his complete identification with those he saves. On the one hand, no other baptism performed by John involved the descent of the Holy Spirit, nor did anyone else baptized by John hear God say, "You are my beloved Son; with you I am well pleased" (Luke 3:22). On the other, Luke's introduction to the episode reminds us that Jesus' baptism was not entirely unique: "Now when all the people were baptized, and when Jesus also had been baptized . . ." (Luke 3:21).

Does this imply that Jesus, like others who received John's baptism, is seeking "forgiveness of sins" (Luke 3:3)? Two factors assure us that this cannot be Luke's meaning. First, John announces that Jesus will baptize others with the *Holy* Spirit, and will carry out judgment on the sins of others (Luke 3:16), two actions that imply a superhuman degree of holiness. Second, as the Spirit descends on Jesus, God declares that he is "well pleased" with his Son (Luke 3:22), recalling Isaiah 42:1: "Behold my servant . . . in whom my soul delights; I have put my Spirit upon him." In other words, God is declaring that Jesus is the Suffering Servant of Isaiah, the innocent sacrifice who will die for the sins of others (Isa. 53:1–12). Jesus' baptism is therefore not an indication that he is sinful and needs to repent, but a sign of his complete identification with God's people—an identification that will ultimately include sharing their sorrows and enduring the punishment they deserve (Isa. 53:4–6). He can suffer in our place because he shares our humanity.

## The Genealogy of the Second Adam: Luke 3:23–38

Luke's record of Jesus' genealogy (Luke 3:23–38) further highlights Jesus' humanity. Readers familiar with Matthew's genealogy (Matt. 1:1–17) will immediately notice the differences in the accounts. Matthew begins with Abraham and proceeds forward through time, naming only forty of Jesus' ancestors (plus Mary). Luke, on the other hand, begins with Jesus and moves backward through time, naming seventy-six of Jesus' ancestors, including "Adam, the son of God" (Luke 3:38). In addition, Matthew traces Jesus' descent from David's son *Solomon*, while Luke refers to David's son *Nathan* instead.

Two factors likely account for the differences in the genealogies. First, recent research argues persuasively that Matthew traces the legal, royal line from David to Joseph, and Luke the actual biological line.[1] In other words, Matthew demonstrates that Jesus, like Solomon, is the rightful *legal* heir to David's

1. For a summary of these and other possible interpretations, see Darrell L. Bock, *Luke*, Baker Exegetical Commentary on the New Testament, 2 vols. (Grand Rapids: Baker, 1994–96), 1:918–23.

throne, while Luke stresses the *biological* ties linking Jesus (through his adopted father, Joseph) to David. Second, the reason the Gospel writers have chosen different approaches to the genealogy is to emphasize complementary truths about Jesus. Matthew's major concern is to demonstrate that Jesus is "the son of David" (Matt. 1:1) who fulfills God's purposes for Israel. Luke agrees with this truth, but uses his genealogy to broaden the scope of Jesus' significance: as one related (through his adopted father, Joseph) not only to David and Abraham but ultimately to Adam, Jesus fulfills God's purposes for humanity, Jew and Gentile alike.

Luke's inclusion of Adam in Jesus' genealogy indicates that in Jesus, the human race has a second beginning. In Jesus, we see a new way of being human; where Adam and all his descendants are faithless, ruled and guided by the power of sin, Jesus will remain faithful, led by the power of God's Holy Spirit. To use a phrase that is typically linked with Paul's theology, Jesus is the "second Adam." While Luke never uses this language, he clearly intends us to read his Gospel with this concept in mind.

## The Temptation of the Second Adam: Luke 4:1–13

Luke 4:1–13 continues this emphasis as it recounts Jesus' temptation in the wilderness. Given the importance of the temptation narrative throughout our study, here we will discuss the text in some detail, especially as it expresses the "second Adam" theme.[2]

After his baptism, Jesus is led by the Holy Spirit into the wilderness; after fasting for forty days, he endures three specific temptations by "the devil," or Satan (Luke 4:2):

2. This text also presents Jesus as the "new Israel" whose faithful obedience contrasts the grumbling and failure of Israel in the wilderness. While we will focus on the second Adam theme, both themes point to Jesus as the perfect embodiment of human faithfulness before God.

- First, Jesus is tempted to satisfy his hunger by his own provision: "If you are the Son of God, command this stone to become bread" (Luke 4:3).
- Next, having been shown all the kingdoms of the world (apparently in a vision), Jesus is tempted to secure power and recognition for himself: "If you . . . will worship me, it will all be yours" (Luke 4:7).
- Finally, the scene shifts to the pinnacle of the temple in Jerusalem, where the devil, quoting portions of Psalm 91, tempts Jesus to prove for himself that God's promises of care for him are trustworthy: "If you are the Son of God, throw yourself down from here, for it is written . . ." (Luke 4:9–11).

In each case, Jesus resists the devil's temptations, replying by citing Scripture texts from the book of Deuteronomy (Deut. 8:3; 6:13; 6:16). Overcome by Jesus, Satan departs "until an opportune time" (Luke 4:13). At this point Luke begins his account of Jesus' public ministry, suggesting that a major purpose of the temptation account is to demonstrate that Jesus is qualified to begin his work as Redeemer.

Readers of this text often have two initial questions. First, could Jesus actually have sinned? That is, are these real temptations, or does Jesus' divinity make him immune to them? And second, why does Luke follow a different order than Matthew, whose account concludes with the temptation to worship Satan? Both questions actually relate to our purpose, which is to observe how Luke's temptation account portrays Jesus as a truly human second Adam. No biblical writer explicitly says whether Jesus could have sinned, or what consequences might have followed if he had; thus Christian theologians have differed over these matters. What is clear from Luke's text is that Jesus is fully human—not sharing Adam's sinfulness, but nonetheless a real human person with a real human body. Like us, he can be tempted to serve himself, save himself, and trust himself rather than his Father. Unlike us, he experiences these temptations as one who has never known sin. Thus the temptation story highlights a key parallel between Jesus and Adam: both are sinless (Adam as a created image-bearer of God, Jesus as the Spirit-conceived Son of God) and yet capable of being tempted.[3]

At the same time, the second Adam faces a challenge more serious than that of the first. Adam was tempted in the setting of the garden of Eden, designed by God as the perfect environment for human life to flourish; Jesus is tempted in the wilderness, a place hostile to human life. At the moment of his temptation, Adam had never known pain, deprivation, or sorrow of any kind; Jesus knows what it is to be hungry (Luke 4:2); to live in a world where false gods, including power and glory, are worshiped (Luke 4:5–7); and to have a body that is susceptible to injury and death (Luke 4:9–11). Adam's rebellious act plunged the human race into death, curse, and alienation from God and neighbor; Jesus' obedience must reopen the way to life, blessing, and love. Thus Luke, like other biblical writers, portrays Jesus' temptations not as a pretense or a show, but as a conflict of cosmic proportions. Jesus, the second Adam, must faithfully face more numerous tests, under harsher conditions, if Adam's failure is to be reversed.

But how can we be sure that Luke wants us to see these points of comparison between Adam and Jesus? The answer lies in the order of the temptations. Most scholars agree on two facts: (1) Matthew's Gospel gives the order in which the temptations actually occurred (bread, temple, worship); and (2) Luke claims only that these three temptations occurred, without stressing

3. For respected theologians taking different sides of the debate over whether Jesus, like Adam, was capable of sinning, see Charles Hodge, *Systematic Theology*, 3 vols. (Grand Rapids: Eerdmans, 1993), 2:457 (Jesus "must have been capable of sinning"); and Louis Berkhof, *Systematic Theology*, 4th ed. (Grand Rapids: Eerdmans, 1988), 318 ("it was impossible for Him to sin").

their chronological sequence.[4] It appears, then, that Luke has used a different sequence in order to draw attention to Satan's questioning of Jesus' divine sonship. In Luke's order, the first and third temptations begin with the phrase, "If you are the Son of God." This emphasis creates a clear link between the temptation account of Luke 4 and the genealogy of Luke 3, which opens with a reminder that Jesus is really not the son of Joseph but the Son of God (compare Luke 3:22 with Luke 3:23), and closes by naming "Adam, the son of God." Together, these texts indicate that Jesus is a second Adam—a new and greater Son of God who, unlike the first "son of God," will faithfully embody God's intention for human living. As the second Adam, Jesus has come to reverse the failures of the first.

Two features of Luke's temptation account suggest that Jesus' entire ministry, and not just his victory in the wilderness, should be viewed as a reversal of Adam's failure. First, Luke 4:13 makes it clear that the wilderness temptation does not represent the final testing of Jesus' faithfulness: "And when the devil had ended every temptation, he departed from [Jesus] until an opportune time." Second, Luke's placement of the temptation to leap from the temple in the third, and climactic, position foreshadows Jesus' coming death in Jerusalem. This suggests that the "opportune time" of Luke 4:13 occurs at the end of Jesus' life, where Jesus is again tested by a threefold temptation to save himself from the agonies of the crucifixion (see Luke 23:35–39). Having resisted these taunts, Jesus promises the repentant thief, "Truly, I say to you, today you will be with me in *Paradise*" (Luke 23:43)—the final term implying that Jesus restores sinners to the kind of relationship with God that existed in the garden of Eden, but was forfeited by Adam's sin.[5] According to Luke's Gospel, then,

4. Note that Matt. 4:5 joins the first and second temptations by "then," implying sequence, whereas Luke joins the various temptations simply with "and."

5. Luke's word *paradeisos* is the preferred term in the Septuagint, the Greek translation of the Old Testament, for referring to the garden of Eden. Paul uses the same

Jesus reverses the failure of the first Adam by living his entire life—up to and including his death—as a completely faithful image-bearer of God. In this role as the faithful second Adam, Jesus is the founder of a new, redeemed race of humanity. But this unique status as founder also makes him, both in his life and in his death, the model, paradigm, and example for all who become a part of that race through faith in him.

## Luke's Portrait of Jesus' Humanity

As we have seen, Luke relates Jesus' baptism, genealogy, and temptation in ways that stress his true humanity. This emphasis is confirmed by several themes that run throughout Luke's Gospel:

1. *Jesus has a physical body with real needs.* Jesus grows fatigued and needs sleep (Luke 8:23), and he relies on others to provide for his material needs (Luke 8:3). Even after his resurrection, Jesus is a real, flesh-and-blood human (Luke 24:39–43).

2. *Jesus enjoys fellowship with others, including its physical expressions.* The theme of table fellowship is especially prominent in Luke. Jesus uses eating and drinking to confirm, establish, and invite relational ties (Luke 5:29–30; 7:34, 36, 49; 11:37; 14:1; 15:2). The comments of Luke 7:44–46 imply that Jesus appreciates physical gestures of hospitality and gratitude.

3. *Jesus expresses a wide range of human emotions.* Jesus gives incarnate, embodied expression to various emotions as he reacts to the realities of human life, including amazement

word in 2 Cor. 12:3, referring not to the garden of Eden, but nevertheless to a place of glorious and intimate knowledge of God.

(Luke 7:9), compassion (Luke 7:13), frustration (Luke 9:41; 11:40; 12:56; 13:15–16; 22:51), determination (Luke 9:51, 53), joy (Luke 10:21), distress (Luke 12:50; 22:44), sorrow (Luke 13:34; 19:41–44), and pity (Luke 23:28–29). Jesus' cleansing of the temple (Luke 19:45–46) may imply anger, and his promise to the repentant thief on the cross (Luke 23:43) suggests that hope sustains Jesus during his crucifixion.

4. *Jesus engages in ordinary expressions of human religious life.* Jesus regularly attends corporate worship (Luke 4:15–16; 13:10), he gives thanks for God's provision of food (Luke 9:16; 22:17), and—an aspect of Jesus' life that receives special attention in Luke's Gospel—he prays (Luke 5:16; 6:12; 9:18; 10:21; 11:1; 22:32; 23:34, 46). Jesus' humanity is especially evident in the garden of Gethsemane (Luke 22:41–44), as he seeks strength for doing the Father's will through prayer.

5. *Jesus experiences suffering, agony, humiliation, and weakness—culminating in his death.* Throughout his life Jesus endures rejection (Luke 8:37; 9:53; 10:16; 12:9–10; 17:25; 19:14; 23:18), derision (Luke 4:22; 5:5; 8:53), mockery (Luke 16:14; 22:63–65; 23:11, 35–39), accusation of sin (Luke 5:21; 6:7; 7:34; 11:15, 45, 53–54; 14:1; 15:2; 19:7; 23:2, 5, 10), and even murderous rage (Luke 4:29; 6:11; 9:22; 13:31; 19:47; 20:14, 19; 22:2; 23:20, 23). He ultimately endures death on a cross, designed not only to physically torment its victims, but to utterly humiliate them (Luke 9:22, 44; 17:25; 18:31–33; 22:63; 23:32–46). Though he is the Son of God, he has a body that must be buried by others—in a borrowed tomb (Luke 23:50–24:3). As a true human being, Jesus knows what it is to be broken by life in a world devastated by sin.

What we have established here, and what we will continue to see throughout our study, is that Jesus is truly human. As one born into our world and experiencing a full range of joys and sorrows—physical, emotional, spiritual, and relational—his humanity is complete, not partial, and actual, not apparent. And as the second Adam, reversing Adam's failure by his faithfulness, Jesus lives as God's image-bearers are intended to live. The Son of God is also a human being who gets being human right.

## Implications for Imitation

We opened this chapter with a question: Who is Jesus? Luke's Gospel affirms both that Jesus is the unique, saving Son of God and that he is truly human. From what we have learned, we may now trace out five implications related to the imitation of Christ.

1. *A proper emphasis on the imitation of Christ must reflect the fuller picture of who Christ is and what he has done.* The testimony of Luke's Gospel is clear: Jesus is the Son of God whose life, death, and resurrection accomplish our salvation. A proper emphasis on Jesus' example will never undermine this truth.

2. *The theological foundation for the imitation of Christ is his true humanity.* Because the Son of God is also fully human, our being like him is not an impossibility. In fact, Luke's portrayal of Jesus as a second Adam invites us to see in Jesus' life and death a pattern for human faithfulness as God has intended it from the beginning. To look to Jesus as a paradigm for faithful human living is not contrary to, but consistent with, Luke's overall purpose.

3. *We must carefully distinguish between those features of Jesus' life that are unique and those features that are part of our shared humanity.* Jesus' prayer in Gethsemane (Luke 22:39–46), which will receive extended treatment in a later chapter, illustrates the principle. On the one hand, this

event is unique, the climactic spiritual struggle of the Son of God as he prepares to lay down his life. On the other, the spiritual dynamics that this prayer expresses—the awful weight of faithfulness, the tension between God's will for us and our will for ourselves—are universally experienced by God's people. In such cases, the themes surveyed in this chapter can help us distinguish the unique aspects of Jesus' life from those which serve as a model for us as his followers.

4. *We may expect Jesus to model the opposite of any sin he criticizes.* The second Adam theme allows us to observe an important principle to which we will return throughout our study: since Jesus faithfully resists temptation, we may expect him to model resistance to any sin which he criticizes in his teaching. If Jesus warns us that love of money is a snare that leads to human failure (e.g., Luke 12:13–34), or that religious devotion can easily turn to hypocrisy (e.g., Luke 11:37–44), we may legitimately ask how he, as the second Adam, models more faithful alternatives.

5. *Love is the fuel for imitation.* Appreciation for Jesus' true humanity, including his faithfulness as the second Adam, should ultimately have the effect of increasing our love for him. When we consider what faithfulness was required of Jesus that we might be restored to "Paradise" (Luke 23:43); when we consider that the circumstances under which he displayed that faithfulness were far more difficult than those faced by the first Adam; and when we consider that his humanity included deeper experience of rejection, humiliation, and suffering than any other person has ever known—how could we fail to love him more? Thus, Luke's portrait of Jesus as the model of true humanity serves both as a call to imitate him, and as fuel

for the love from which that imitation flows—a concept to which we will return in chapter 13.

## Conclusion

Back at the wedding, I had a chance to ask the flower girl a question of my own. "Have you ever heard of Jesus?" When she answered, "No," I was able to tell her a story about God's goodness, about his anger and sadness at our disobedience, and his wise plan to put everything right again by sending his Son into our world. Luke's Gospel is more detailed, and it uses a more sophisticated vocabulary, but it too tells this same story, the story to which everyone must listen before they can become imitators of Christ. In our next chapter, we will learn more about how Luke intends us to read this story, and what impact he intends it to have on us. As he did for my friend the flower girl, may God give us wise and attentive hearts so that we might become better at listening to Luke—and at following Jesus.

# 4

# Getting Oriented, Part II: Foundations for Studying Imitation in Luke

CAN YOU IMAGINE what it would be like if the Gospels came with an instruction book—or, to use a more current image, a "helpline" complete with a phone menu? "Thank you for choosing to read Luke's Gospel," a prerecorded voice might say. "To better understand what it means to trust Jesus as Savior, press 1. To better understand Jesus' teaching, press 2. To better understand how to follow Jesus' example, press 3." We scratch our heads, not quite sure these three options can be so neatly separated. But eventually, given our interest in the topic of this book—*beep*—we press three. "Thank you for choosing to follow Jesus' example. For more proof that you *should* follow his example, press 1. For a list of ways to be like Jesus, press 2. For help keeping the list from getting ridiculous, press 3."

Now the choice is harder. The skeptic in us may want to press 1, but the pragmatist in us wants to press 2. Yet there is something intriguing about option 3. Surely there's a way to distinguish proper applications of the imitation of Christ from those that just seem silly. Am I really being like Jesus if I grow a beard, wear a white robe, eat a "Jesus diet," or learn to sing Psalms in Hebrew? After a little wrestling, another *beep*—we press two. "There are 438 ways that you should be like Jesus. For numbers 1–50, press 1. For numbers 51–100, press 2. For numbers 101–150 . . ."

While this scenario is far-fetched, it represents three very real concerns that the present chapter will address. First, we want to be sure that Luke intended us to read his Gospel with the imitation of Christ in mind. Earlier chapters have provided some reasons to believe that this is the case, but given the combination of suspicion and sloppiness with which the topic has been handled in Protestant circles, it will be helpful to summarize more evidence. Second, we want to be able to distinguish those features of Jesus' character and conduct that Luke does intend us to imitate from those he does not. We will therefore review four interpretive guidelines that will form the foundation for the rest of our study. Finally, we want to be able to pinpoint the ways in which we are called to be like Jesus. However, if the result is an overwhelming number of new priorities for daily living, we will be paralyzed and wearied by our study rather than strengthened and encouraged. To address this concern, this chapter will conclude with an overview of four principles that will provide a framework not only for the remainder of this book, but for our daily pursuit of likeness to Christ.

## Starting Points: Evidence for Imitation in Luke

Three particular features of Luke's Gospel convince us that the imitation of Christ is one of its intended emphases. One is reflected in a key verse that is unique to Luke, and two are characteristic of the Gospel as a whole.

### *Imitation and Discipleship: Luke 6:40*

In Luke 6:39–42, Jesus warns his hearers against the sins of hypocrisy and presumption, and against choosing spiritual guides characterized by such sins. Someone who cannot tell the difference between a "speck" and a "log"—and who claims to see the "speck" in another's eye despite the "log" in his own—is not a trustworthy teacher. The danger in following such teachers is that we eventually become like those who lead us. In Luke 6:39, Jesus makes this point metaphorically: if your guide falls into a pit, you will end up in the pit as well. In Luke 6:40, he repeats the point more plainly: "A disciple is not above his teacher, but everyone when he is fully trained will be like his teacher."

At first glance, this verse doesn't promise much for our study. In its context, the verse sounds less like a call to imitate Jesus as our true teacher, and more like a warning against following teachers who specialize in trivial matters (like the Pharisees and scribes Jesus has encountered in Luke 5–6). What is instructive about this verse, however, is what it assumes. Its very form—a generic, proverbial statement, with no supporting argument—suggests that Jesus and his hearers would have viewed it as uncontroversial. Jesus lived, and Luke wrote, in a world where people expected their lives to be shaped by the example of their teachers!

This is not always the case in today's world. In contemporary Western culture, teaching is often a matter of information transfer: if your students do well on exams, you may be called a good "teacher," even if you have made no effort to impact their hearts and lives at a deeper level. In Jesus' world, expectations regarding teaching were radically different. Jewish rabbis, for instance, were expected not only to communicate an accurate understanding of Scripture, but to convey a way of life that would embody scriptural teaching. Disciples expected their teachers to provide answers to significant questions about applying God's law—but they expected these answers to come just as much from a teacher's example as from his words. As Swedish scholar Birger Gerhardsson puts it, "[The disciple] does not only say, 'I heard from my teacher,' but also 'I saw my teacher do this or that.'"[1] What was true among Jewish rabbis and their disciples was also true among Greek and Roman philosophers and their pupils. In Jesus' world, whether among Jews or Gentiles, to teach was to put your life on display so that students might learn by imitating one wiser than themselves.

It is significant, then, that fourteen times in Luke's Gospel Jesus is said to "teach"—most often in synagogues (Luke 4:15, 31; 6:6; 13:10, 22) or in the temple courts (Luke 19:47; 20:1; 21:37)—and thirteen times he is referred to as "teacher"—most often by his critics (Luke 7:40; 11:45; 19:39; 20:21, 28, 39) or by leaders who reject his responses to their questions (Luke 10:25; 18:18). This underscores the ongoing tension between Jesus and Jewish religious leaders; all are "teachers," but they offer two competing visions of God, his kingdom, and his priorities. Thus when Luke 6:40 warns us against following hypocritical teachers lest we become like them, it implies that Jesus is the true teacher we *should* follow, and like whom we *should* be. Any reader familiar with Jewish culture would therefore conclude that Jesus' disciples should imitate his example.

### *Imitation and Ancient Biography*

Further confirmation that Luke intends his readers to imitate Jesus comes from the fact that his Gospel shares many features in common with Greco-Roman biographies. For instance, such biographies (known in ancient times as *bioi*, "lives") are narratives about a central figure whose words and deeds are continually

1. Birger Gerhardsson, *Memory and Manuscript: Oral Tradition and Written Transmission in Rabbinic Judaism and Early Christianity* (Lund: Gleerup and Copenhagen: Munksgaard, 1961), 183, quoted in Michael Griffiths, *The Example of Jesus*, The Jesus Library (Downers Grove, IL: InterVarsity Press, 1985), 23.

in focus, and whose death represents the culmination of his character, beliefs, and accomplishments.[2] This is not to say that Luke's Gospel is a biography, for it also shares many features in common with Old Testament historical books. Thus, unlike Greco-Roman writers of "lives," Luke is not interested in Jesus simply because he is a noble or noteworthy figure, but because he is the Messiah who continues and completes the story of God's redeeming work. Still, there are enough parallels to suggest that there is overlap between Luke's aims and the aims of ancient "lives"—one of which was to encourage readers to imitate the character of the central figure. The Greek rhetorician Isocrates, for example, introduces his "life" of a deceased ruler with the comment that "we exhort young men to the study of philosophy by praising others in order that they, emulating those who are eulogized, may desire to adopt the same pursuits."[3] Nearer the time of the New Testament, Plutarch, one of the most prolific writers of *bioi*, says that he writes in order to use "history as a mirror . . . endeavouring in a manner to fashion and adorn my life in conformity with the virtues" of his subjects; subsequent comments make it clear that Plutarch wants his readers to do the same.[4]

In light of these backgrounds, it is no wonder Jesus could say—without argument—that "everyone when he is fully trained will be like his teacher." For Luke's readers, reading a document that was *like* an ancient biography and *about* a Jewish teacher,

2. This paragraph draws heavily on the work of Richard A. Burridge, especially his *Imitating Jesus: An Inclusive Approach to New Testament Ethics* (Grand Rapids and Cambridge: Eerdmans, 2007), 23–31. While Burridge's insights are helpful, he tends to overemphasize the similarities of the Gospels to ancient *bioi*, without adequately accounting for the distinctions.

3. Isocrates, *Evagoras* 77, in *Isocrates III*, trans. Larue Van Hook, Loeb Classical Library 373 (repr.; Cambridge, MA: Harvard University Press and London: Heinemann, 1961).

4. Plutarch, *Timoleon* 1, in *Plutarch's Lives VI*, trans. Bernadotte Perrin, Loeb Classical Library 98 (repr.; Cambridge, MA: Harvard University Press and London: Heinemann, 1961).

the implication would have been clear: Jesus wants his followers to be "fully trained," and therefore to be like him.

### *Imitation and the Prescriptive-Descriptive Pattern in Luke*

A final feature of Luke that encourages the imitation of Jesus' example is the constant interplay of *prescriptive* and *descriptive* elements. Prescriptive texts are those that prescribe behavior—that is, they call for a response on the part of characters/readers through a direct command of Jesus or some other authority (e.g., God, an angel, or Scripture). Luke 3:8, for example, is a prescriptive text, with John the Baptist, a prophet of God, issuing a direct command: "Bear fruits in keeping with repentance." By contrast, descriptive texts are less direct, calling readers to respond to spiritual truth by portraying characters who embody, or fail to embody, a proper response to that truth. Luke 19:8, for instance, addresses the issue of repentance by describing Zacchaeus and his joyful declaration to Jesus: "Behold, Lord, the half of my goods I give to the poor. And if I have defrauded anyone of anything, I restore it fourfold." This text does not explicitly tell anyone to do anything; but it does call for a response by raising important questions: What would it look like to act in a way that gives evidence of repentance? How might a repentant person begin to handle money differently?

Consider two further examples of descriptive texts:

- *Luke 7:30*: Luke's comment that "the Pharisees and lawyers rejected the purpose of God for themselves" is purely descriptive. It never says, "Reader, beware! Do not reject God's purpose by failing to repent!" In fact, it doesn't have to. Any reader can understand that these leaders are modeling folly, and that Jesus—and Luke—intends us to do the opposite.

- *Luke 21:1–4*: Jesus' comment on the poor widow who puts "all she had to live on" in an offering box at the temple is purely descriptive. Jesus does not say, "She clearly trusts God to provide for her needs, and you should too." But when we interpret this text in light of prescriptive texts on anxiety (Luke 12:22–34), love of money (Luke 12:13–21; 16:1–15), and God's promises to the poor (Luke 6:20), it is clear that the widow embodies an appropriate response to the gospel.

As these few examples demonstrate, there are no value-neutral descriptions in Luke's Gospel. We are intended to read descriptive texts in light of the prescriptive, so that explicit calls for response tune our ears to hear the implicit calls as well. This confirms that Luke intends us to read narratives *about Jesus* on two levels: first, as descriptions of how Jesus brings redemption to a lost world, fulfilling God's saving purpose; and second, as depictions of what a life aligned with that purpose looks like. Of course, Jesus does not model every aspect of our duty; for instance, he does not repent of sin, trust himself, or submit to his own authority. But the broader point still stands: Luke's narratives about Jesus, like narratives about other characters, implicitly call us to imitate him.

## Interpretive Guidelines: Hearing the Call to Imitate Christ

Clearly, we should read Luke's Gospel with the imitation of Christ in mind. But how will we identify which features of Christ's life we are intended to imitate? We will briefly discuss four guidelines that help us to answer this question.

### *Correspondence between Jesus' Teaching and Life*

Where there is correspondence between what Jesus requires of his followers and some feature of his own character or conduct, we may conclude that he is functioning as an example for us. This approach is consistent with Luke 6:40, which reminds us to expect Jesus to "practice what he preaches," and with the prescriptive-descriptive interplay observed above. We see such correspondence between Jesus' command to "love your enemies" (6:35) and his prayer for his crucifiers ("Father, forgive them," Luke 23:34); between his command to leave house and family for the sake of God's kingdom (Luke 18:29) and the fact that "the Son of Man has nowhere to lay his head" (Luke 9:58); and between his instruction on prayer (e.g., Luke 11:2–13) and the many references in Luke to Jesus' own prayers (e.g., Luke 11:1).

Lack of such correspondence helps us to make important distinctions. For instance, Jesus' prayer before appointing the twelve apostles (Luke 6:12) teaches us to depend on God for wisdom; but since Jesus nowhere teaches that others should appoint apostles, we do not imitate him in this. Similarly, we do not attempt to imitate Jesus' interactions with demons; while he does give authority over demons to the Twelve (Luke 9:1), he does not teach that all believers possess such authority.[5] As these two examples suggest, where such correspondence is lacking, we are often dealing with actions that express Jesus' divine authority or his unique calling as Messiah.

### *Contrast between Jesus and False Patterns of Leadership*

Much of Luke's Gospel focuses on Jesus' criticism of false leaders. As we have seen, Luke 6:40, which calls for a fully trained disciple to be like his teacher, is part of Jesus' warning against blind guides and hypocrites. Similarly, when Jesus calls the apostles to servant-leadership by appealing to his own example, he

5. While we may pray against demons, we dare not imitate Jesus' practice of issuing authoritative commands to them. For a helpful summary of responsible Christian engagement with Satan and the demonic, see chapter 10 of Gregory A. Boyd, *God at War: The Bible and Spiritual Conflict* (Downers Grove, IL: InterVarsity Press, 1997).

is responding to the sinful preoccupation with greatness which characterizes not only Gentile rulers but the apostles themselves (Luke 22:24–27). Two conclusions follow: (1) we may expect Jesus to embody the opposite of any character traits or behavior patterns he criticizes in other leaders; (2) where we see such a contrast between Jesus and other leaders, Luke intends us to see Jesus as a role model to be imitated.

Luke 7:36–50 illustrates the point. When "a woman of the city, who was a sinner" enters the house of Simon the Pharisee, there could not be a sharper contrast between the attitudes of Simon and Jesus toward her. The former is merciless, haughty, and repulsed by her presence, while the latter is forgiving, affirming, and happy to receive her. While the text has many functions (e.g., teaching us about the character of God, forgiveness, repentance, and the relationship between salvation and works), one of them is to call us to relate to repentant sinners as Jesus does. Does this mean that we, like Jesus, are to pronounce forgiveness of others' sins (Luke 7:48)? No, because neither this text nor any other faults Pharisees for failing to pronounce the forgiveness of sins; rather, the text faults Simon for failing to recognize and rejoice in forgiveness that God has granted through Jesus. Proper attention to the contrast between Jesus and other leaders enables us to hear the call to imitate him, while reminding us that he is more than a mere example.

### *Consistency with the Purpose of Luke's Gospel*

The question of the purpose of Luke's Gospel (and Acts) is a complex one, to which the attention of many scholars has been devoted. Since space does not allow for an in-depth discussion, I will offer my own summary, which attempts to account for the major themes of both Luke and Acts, and to synthesize the strengths of various scholarly proposals.[6]

6. This synthesis owes much to chapter 2 of H. Douglas Buckwalter, *The Character and Purpose of Luke's Christology*, Society for New Testament Studies Monograph

Simply put, Luke's purpose is to promote the worldwide mission of the church by assuring readers that Jesus is the fulfillment of God's saving plan. This plan is (1) to establish an everlasting kingdom under the reign of the Messiah, who will (2) restore many—Jews and Gentiles alike—to right relationship to God through repentance and the forgiveness of sins, in order (3) to bring the blessings of salvation through Israel into all the world.

To achieve this purpose, Luke must address four paradoxes that could undermine readers' assurance of the truth about Jesus:

- *The Paradox of Rejection*—how can Jesus be the Messiah if he was crucified, and continues to be rejected by so many?
- *The Paradox of Reversal*—why is the Christian message better received among sinners, outcasts, and "unclean" Gentiles than among religious leaders, teachers, and others who scrupulously observe God's law?
- *The Paradox of Reward*—why do those who are most closely aligned with God's saving purpose endure the greatest humiliation and suffering?
- *The Paradox of Progress*—how can the worldwide mission of the church, with its gospel about a crucified Messiah, led by weak and inadequate men, and besieged by conflict and persecution, ever hope to succeed?

In short, Luke's purpose is to help the church spread the good news that Jesus is the Savior of the world, no matter how challenging it may seem to embrace this truth.

---

Series 89 (Cambridge: Cambridge University Press, 1996). Buckwalter himself argues that one of Luke's primary purposes is to present "*the servanthood of the Lord Jesus as the ethical model for Christian living*" (281, emphasis original).

Familiarity with this purpose establishes boundaries for the imitation of Christ. For instance, we reject the idea that we should imitate Jesus by growing a beard or eating a "Jesus diet" not because this sounds silly, but because nothing in Luke or Acts connects such matters to Luke's purpose. The imitation of Christ is not concerned with any and all likeness to Jesus, but with being like him in ways that advance God's saving plan, and in ways that embody the sorts of paradoxes we see in Jesus' life. Likewise, we may rule in bounds those appeals to Jesus' example that *do reflect the core concerns* of Luke's purpose. Jesus' healing miracles illustrate the point. While we cannot assume that people who are growing in Christlikeness will be able to perform miracles like his, it is consistent with Luke's purpose, and with God's saving plan, to say (1) that, like Jesus, all Christians should be concerned to see others liberated from the effects of sin, and (2) that this concern should extend to the relief of physical suffering. Put another way, when we take part in the worldwide mission of the church, we become agents of redemption, who will necessarily reflect the image of redemption's chief Agent.

### *The Principle/Practice Distinction*

A final interpretive guideline that helps us determine how we should imitate Jesus' example involves the distinction between principles and practices. An episode from Acts 1 helps us to appreciate the distinction. Recognizing the need for one of Jesus' close companions to replace Judas, the church does two things: they pray for God's guidance (Acts 1:24–25), and they cast lots (Acts 1:26). Though this is a descriptive text, we have seen that it may still bear hortatory force. But what is it urging us to do? If it is urging us to adopt specific practices, we might conclude that church leaders today should be chosen by rolling dice or flipping coins—but only after a one-sentence prayer has been offered. If, however, we think in terms of principles, we might reach more general conclusions: we should pray for guidance at key moments in the life of the church; we should select leaders through a combination of dependence on God and more tangible, "natural" means; we should trust that God's providence directs every event in the universe, even those that seem random. My own study of the New Testament suggests that where descriptive texts present patterns for our imitation, the focus is on principles rather than on practices. This allows for the truths of Scripture to be applied to a wide range of circumstances, in a vast array of cultural settings.

We see this, for instance, in the way that the New Testament epistles appeal to the example of Jesus. Even though the believers Peter addresses are not being crucified, they may look to Jesus' example as they endure undeserved insults, accusations, and punishments (1 Peter 2:21–23). Similarly, John reasons from Jesus' death on our behalf to our duty to meet the material needs of fellow Christians (1 John 3:16–17); Jesus' example of self-sacrificial love establishes a principle that must be applied through a wide range of practices. Luke 9:23 suggests that Jesus employs similar logic, as he challenges every disciple to "take up his cross *daily* and follow me." Since no one can literally be crucified every day, Jesus has in mind a principle that is reflected in, but broader than, the particular practice of carrying a crossbeam. With this in mind, we will read Luke's Gospel with a focus on how Jesus models broad principles that we can apply in our day-to-day circumstances.[7] As the final section of this chapter shows, our focus will be on four principles in particular.

## Orienting Principles: Four Priorities for the Imitation of Christ

At some point, each of us has experienced "supermarket amnesia." We leave home with a short list of groceries we need

7. The one point at which the New Testament does call for precise repetition of a particular action performed by Jesus is the celebration of the Lord's Supper.

to pick up: milk, bread, cereal, and a few apples. But we walk into the local SuperMegaFood Center, and we're overwhelmed with thousands of varieties of food. Among the dozens of fruits in the produce section, there are ten or more varieties of apples. On the cereal aisle, there are more colors, sizes, and textures than we can count. And so the amnesia sets in; overwhelmed by too many options, we forget why we even came to the store.

Growth toward spiritual maturity can seem this way at times. If we are constantly adding new spiritual priorities to our lives—be more joyful, more generous, more kind, more compassionate, more holy, more pure, more devoted, more disciplined—we can become so frustrated that we don't make any progress at all. Jesus seems to recognize the need for a realistic set of spiritual priorities when he summarizes all of God's commandments under two headings: love God with your whole self, and love your neighbor as yourself (Matt. 22:35–40; Mark 12:28–31; Luke 10:25–28). Jesus does not mean that these are the only commandments that matter, so that others can be ignored. Rather, he intends us to view every other command through this twofold lens, so that every one of God's laws, applied in each of life's circumstances, comes into its proper focus.

Drawing on Jesus' wisdom, we need a practical approach to imitating his example. On the one hand, this approach needs to be clear and simple, so that it is able to reorient us when we are overwhelmed and drifting from true priorities. On the other, our approach must be profound and comprehensive, so that it can account for the complexities of reflecting Jesus' character in all the details of daily life. The image that helps me to envision such an approach is a compass. On the one hand, it is simple, based on only four cardinal directions: north, south, east, and west. On the other, it allows for an infinite variety of applications. Correctly combining those four directions, we can move from any point on the face of our planet to any other point.

Sometimes we go north; sometimes we go north-northwest at a bearing of 332 degrees; and sometimes we go due east for twelve miles, then southwest at a bearing of 218 degrees for forty miles. It all depends on where we are starting from, and where we need to go. But how we get there never changes—always through a combination of north, south, east, and west.

My study of Luke's Gospel suggests that when it comes to the imitation of Christ, there are four cardinal directions, four major principles that oriented Jesus' life and that should orient ours as well:

- Passion for the glory of God
- Passion for the good of other people
- Willing denial of self
- Patient endurance of hardship

As we consider these four principles, several observations are in order. First, while Luke never lists these principles for us, they do provide a helpful way of organizing themes that are prominent in his depiction of Jesus. Second, as later chapters will demonstrate in more detail, each of these topics is a major feature of Jesus' teaching. We will not be surprised, then, to see that Jesus embodies the same principles he requires of others. Third, these four principles provide us with a Christlike orientation to all of life, describing how we are to relate to God, to other people, to ourselves, and to our circumstances. These distinctions provide guidelines for the chapters that follow, in which we will take up each principle in turn, asking how Luke portrays Jesus' relationship to God and how we might imitate his example, how Luke portrays Jesus' interactions with and attitudes toward other people and how we might imitate his example, and so forth. Finally, while these four orienting principles may be distinguished, they cannot ultimately be separated.

Thus, in various chapters we will often return to the same texts to view them from different perspectives. In particular, we will examine Luke's passion narrative multiple times, as Jesus' last hours represent the culmination of each of these principles in his own life, and the most powerful call for us to imitate the example of our Savior.

It is, of course, possible to sit in the comfort of our own homes studying maps and reading websites about how to operate a compass. But the whole point of having a compass is to *go somewhere*, to pick a destination and travel toward it with the confidence that you will not lose your way. As we more deeply explore Luke's portrayal of Jesus' example, and what it would look like for us to reflect that example in our own lives, it is my prayer that two things would happen: first, that we will *go somewhere*, making progress toward the goal of likeness to Christ; and second, that we would come to appreciate more than ever the truth that when we walk in the footsteps of our Savior, we are never in danger of losing our way.

# 5

# Jesus' Passion for the Glory of God

THE NEEDLE OF A COMPASS always points north. For this reason, even though every compass displays four cardinal directions, north has pride of place. As the previous chapter indicated, the remainder of this book will explore four traits that orient Jesus' character and conduct, traits that should be imitated by all of his followers. Yet we will begin our exploration by focusing on the trait that fuels and energizes all the others—namely, Jesus' passion for the glory of God.

## What Is Passion for the Glory of God?

Unfortunately, phrases like "passion for the glory of God" can easily become pious jargon, the sort of thing we might say to sound spiritual without really understanding what we mean. Thankfully, we can understand what it means to speak of passion for God's glory by pondering peaches. Not the rock-hard, flavorless variety available in most grocery stores, but real peaches—South Carolina peaches (I freely confess my bias), soft and juicy and so delicious it almost hurts! If I were to call such a peach "glorious," I would be commenting on its goodness, its excellence, its ability to draw pleasure and delight out of anybody who tastes it, smells it, feels its fuzzy skin, or looks at its vivid shades of orange, yellow, and red. And I would be implying that it is wrong to eat such a perfect fruit and respond by shrugging your shoulders and saying, "Eh. I've had better. And I still prefer black jelly beans anyway." Instead, the right response to glory begins with delight—in this case, smacking lips and juice-covered fingers and a smile that comes from the inside out—and then moves us beyond personal pleasure, so that we want others to share our joy. This is why my summer has involved helping to cook peach cobbler for friends, giving bags of peaches to neighbors, and writing about peaches in a book that has nothing to do with fruit!

God's glory is his excellence, his greatness, his splendor, to which our hearts were designed to respond with worship, reverence, and undivided love. To have passion for his glory means to personally delight in him, and therefore in the gifts he provides, the commands he gives, and the calling to which he appoints us. Yet such passion also includes a longing to see others magnify him by acknowledging and enjoying his greatness with us. In this chapter, therefore, our focus will be on how Luke's Gospel presents Jesus as a model of passion for God's glory, expressed both in his own devotion to his Father and in his commitment to calling others to recognize, and enabling them to enjoy, his Father's greatness.

## Three Reasons to Look to Jesus' Example

In chapter 4 we highlighted several lines of evidence indicating that Luke intends us to see Jesus as an example to be imitated. Here, we want to ask whether Luke intends us to look to Jesus as an example of passion for God's glory in particular. Three features of his Gospel confirm that the answer is "yes."

### *Jesus' Teaching*

First, Jesus teaches that such passion should characterize the life of every person. When a Jewish scribe suggests that to "love the Lord your God with all your heart and with all your soul and with all your strength and with all your mind" is the greatest of human duties before God, Jesus agrees that this is correct (Luke 10:27–28). Jesus makes the same point elsewhere using money as a metaphor: just as coins with Caesar's image imprinted on them should be given to Caesar, so all human beings, with God's "likeness" imprinted on us, should render our whole selves to God (Luke 20:24–25). Similarly, when Jesus teaches his followers how to pray, he begins with two petitions: "Father, hallowed be your name. Your kingdom come" (Luke 11:2). According to Jesus, every disciple should place daily priority on recognizing—and praying that others might recognize—God's holiness and his sovereign, life-giving rule. As we saw in chapter 4, it is right to expect Jesus to reflect the same priorities he requires of others. If Jesus teaches that wholehearted devotion to God is a priority for us, then we can expect Jesus to model such devotion as well.

### *Jesus versus Hypocritical Leaders*

Second, Luke's Gospel frequently contrasts Jesus with other leaders whose devotion to God is insincere or misguided. This sustained contrast invites us to see Jesus not as a "blind guide" whose false piety will lead us into a pit, but as a model of true devotion to God. For example, when Jesus criticizes the Pharisees for loving "what is exalted among men" though it is "an abomination in the sight of God" (Luke 16:15), the implication is that Jesus himself loves what God loves and hates what God hates. It is this true commitment to God, who loves extending forgiveness and mercy to repentant sinners, that causes Jesus to eat with tax collectors and sinners while the Pharisees grumble (Luke 15:1–32; see also Luke 18:9–14).

The contrast between Jesus and false leaders is especially strong in Luke 11:37–52 and Luke 20:45–47. In these texts, Jesus condemns Pharisees and scribes for: (1) emphasizing minor points of God's law while neglecting "justice and the love of God" (Luke 11:42); (2) using their positions of spiritual leadership to gain recognition and status; and (3) spiritually defiling—and even financially defrauding—those who trust their apparent wisdom and biblical expertise. The strength of Jesus' denunciations reflects his own passionate devotion to God. Similarly, recurring disputes over Sabbath observance pit Jesus against leaders who know God's Word but ignore God's purposes, allowing them to emphasize obedience at the expense of mercy (Luke 6:1–11; 13:10–17; 14:1–6). When Jesus confronts such hypocrisy (see Luke 13:15, "You hypocrites!"), we are to see him as a model of genuine commitment to God; like Jesus, we should be concerned with both the requirements of Scripture and its merciful purposes.

### *Jesus and the Worship of God*

Third, Luke characterizes Jesus as one who is passionate about the glory of God by linking Jesus' presence with the worship of God. As Mary anticipates Jesus' birth, she "magnifies the Lord" (Luke 1:46); when Jesus is born, angels sing, "Glory to God in the highest" (Luke 2:14), and the shepherds return to their fields "glorifying and praising God" (Luke 2:19). Similarly, the Gospel closes by noting that after Jesus' ascension, the apostles "were continually in the temple blessing God" (Luke 24:53). Between these "bookend" texts, many of Jesus' miracles lead observers to worship God:

- *Luke 5:25–26*: Having been accused of blasphemy, Jesus heals a paralytic; as a result, both the paralytic and the crowd "glorify" God.

- *Luke 8:39*: Jesus instructs the healed Gerasene demoniac to go home and "declare how much God has done for you;" in response the man tells "the whole city how much Jesus had done for him."
- *Luke 9:43*: When Jesus heals a boy by casting out an unclean spirit, onlookers are "astonished at the majesty of God."
- *Luke 13:10–13*: After Jesus heals a woman with a "disabling spirit," she glorifies God.
- *Luke 17:15–17*: Jesus commends a Samaritan leper who responds to his healing by "praising God" and thanking Jesus.
- *Luke 18:43*: A blind man healed by Jesus follows him, "glorifying God," leading others to give "praise to God."
- *Luke 19:37*: At the triumphal entry, a "multitude" of Jesus' disciples praise God for the mighty works Jesus has done.

In drawing conclusions from such texts, we have to take into account Jesus' unique status as God's Son; the "mighty works" Jesus does are accomplished by his divine power, and only he can rightly share in the worship offered to God. Still, by showing us that Jesus consistently acts in ways that call and enable others to magnify God, Luke's Gospel suggests that anyone who follows Jesus must be motivated by a similar passion for the glory of God.

## Jesus' Passion at the Temple

Sunsets are glorious, no matter where we are when we see them. Still, most of us recognize that there are special places we can visit—a mountainside, the beach, an open prairie with its endless horizon—to see the beauty of a sunset displayed in spectacular ways. In the same way, while the whole of Luke's

Gospel reflects Jesus' passion for God's glory, we need to visit four locations where Luke sheds special light on this aspect of his character.

We begin at the temple in Jerusalem, where Luke gives us our first opportunity to observe Jesus' actions and words. At the age of twelve, Jesus has gone with his parents to Jerusalem to celebrate the Passover (Luke 2:41–42). While Joseph and Mary return to Nazareth, believing Jesus to be with other family and friends on the road, Jesus remains in the temple, "sitting among the teachers, listening to them and asking them questions" (Luke 2:46). Mary's first question for Jesus suggests that he has been disobedient and unloving: "Son, why have you treated us so?" (Luke 2:48). Jesus' response—"Did you not know that I must be in my Father's house?" (Luke 2:49)—makes it clear that Jesus has not been disobeying his earthly parents, but honoring his heavenly Father. The end of the account confirms that Jesus has not been in the wrong: even though he comprehends the situation more clearly than Mary and Joseph (Luke 2:50), he submits to their authority (Luke 2:51).

What does this event reveal of Jesus' character? First, it shows us that he obediently submits to God's purpose for his life. The phrase "I must be" (Luke 2:49; more literally, "it is necessary for me to be") expresses a sense of necessity and obligation; that is, Jesus believes it would be wrong for him to be anywhere other than where God wants him to be. Second, Jesus' interaction with teachers in the temple shows us that he desires to understand Scripture. While he already displays more understanding than would be expected of a child his age (Luke 2:47), Jesus is eager to know more. He is glad to be in his Father's house, learning more about his Father's purposes, from his Father's Word.

The remainder of Luke's Gospel reinforces this portrait, as Jesus often speaks of an obligation to carry out God's purposes in fulfillment of Scripture. In Luke 4:43, for example, Jesus refuses to stay in Capernaum, saying, "I *must* preach the good news of the kingdom of God to the other towns as well; for I was sent for this purpose." Because he is the Son of Man who came to seek and to save the lost (Luke 19:10), he "must" stay at Zacchaeus's house (Luke 19:5). On two occasions Jesus tells his disciples that the Son of Man "must" suffer and die before being raised (Luke 9:22; 17:25), and after his resurrection he rebukes two disciples on the road to Emmaus for failing to recognize from Scripture that it was "necessary" for the Christ to suffer before entering his glory (Luke 24:26). Among his final instructions to the apostles is a reminder that "everything written about me . . . must be fulfilled" (Luke 24:44; see also Luke 22:37). From the first time we meet him as a twelve-year-old until after his resurrection, Jesus glorifies God by turning to Scripture in order to understand and fulfill his Father's purpose.

Before moving from the temple to our next location, we need to reflect on what this episode does and does not teach us about imitating Christ. On the one hand, we could read the text with such an emphasis on its uniqueness that imitation becomes impossible. After all, the scenario it presents—a preadolescent boy and his earthly parents grappling with the requirements of a third "parent," God himself, in the context of that boy's mission to redeem the world—will never be repeated. On the other hand, the text provides fodder for moralizing: "Children should willingly go to church. Parents should understand that God may call children to unexpected forms of obedience. Twelve-year-olds should join discussion groups with religious leaders." A healthier perspective avoids these extremes. We recognize that the text is unique in many of its aspects, so that we should not attempt to convert every detail into contemporary application. But we also recognize that the text underscores a principle that characterizes Jesus' entire life, and which makes him a model for us—namely, his passion for honoring God.

## Jesus' Passion in the Wilderness

The second place we must visit is the wilderness of Luke 4:1–13, where Jesus is tempted by Satan. While we will return to this multifaceted text in later chapters to reflect on other character traits, here we focus on how the text portrays Jesus as a model of wholehearted commitment to God. First, however, we need to remember that this text combines the unique and the exemplary. Jesus' testing is unique in that it is the final preparation for his public ministry as Messiah, a once-for-all demonstration that he is ready for his redemptive mission. John Calvin, frustrated with the medieval Roman Catholic Church's use of this text to call believers to a forty-day fast during Lent, made this point well:

> [I]t is plain that Christ did not fast to set an example for others, but to prove, in so beginning to proclaim the gospel, that it was no human doctrine but actually one sent from heaven. . . . For Christ does not fast often—as he would have to do if he had willed to lay down a law of yearly fasting—but only once, when he girded himself for the proclamation of the gospel. Nor does he fast in human fashion [that is, for a more typical period of time], as would have been fitting if he willed to arouse men to imitate him.[1]

At the same time, we have seen that this text portrays Jesus as the second Adam, the perfect embodiment of faithful human living. For this reason, we recognize in it a call not to particular practices (such as wilderness retreats or extended fasts), but to principles of Christlike character, including devotion to God.

How then does Jesus' wilderness temptation portray him as a model of passionate commitment to God? In the first place,

1. John Calvin, *Institutes of the Christian Religion*, 2 vols., ed. John T. McNeill, The Library of Christian Classics, vol. 20 (Louisville, London, and Leiden: Westminster John Knox, 1960), 4.12.20.

like the account of the boy Jesus in the temple, it shows us that *Jesus is devoted to God's Word*. He rebuffs each temptation with a quotation from Scripture, indicating not only that he knows Scripture well, but that he turns to it as a source of strength in trial. Though Jesus quotes only the negative principle in response to Satan's first temptation, he has clearly embraced both of the principles expressed in Deuteronomy 8:3: "man does not live by bread alone, but man lives by every word that comes from the mouth of the Lord." Second, the temptation narrative shows us that *Jesus keeps God's commandments because he trusts God's provision*. As the context of Deuteronomy 8:3 makes clear, God tested Israel's willingness to keep his commandments by calling them to trust him to supply their material needs during the wilderness wandering (Deut. 8:2–4). In fact, the chapter later warns that material prosperity can lead to idolatrous pride: "Beware lest you say in your heart, 'My power and the might of my hand have gotten me this wealth'" (Deut. 8:17). By refusing to provide for himself by turning stones to bread, Jesus demonstrates his dependent, obedient spirit. Jesus the faithful Son, the new Israel, the second Adam, delights to trust the power and might of his Father's hand, not his own.

Third, Luke's temptation narrative teaches us that *Jesus loves God, and God alone, with all his heart*; as a result, fourth, *he loves God's honor more than his own*. When he is tempted to secure honor for himself—the "authority" and "glory" of "all the kingdoms of the world" (Luke 4:5–6)—by worshiping Satan, Jesus replies by quoting Deuteronomy 6:13: "You shall worship the Lord your God, and him only shall you serve" (Luke 4:8).[2] Again, the Old Testament context sheds light on Jesus' commitment to God. As Deuteronomy 6 opens, we hear the great commandment

2. Luke 4:8 differs slightly from Deut. 6:13. Where the OT text refers to *fearing* God, Jesus refers to *worshiping* God, apparently echoing the language of Satan's temptation ("If you . . . will worship me."). And Jesus uses the word "only," which, though not in the OT text, is certainly implied by the OT context.

to "love the Lord your God with all your heart and with all your soul and with all your might" (Deut. 6:5). Israel is then warned that the prosperity God has promised—cities and houses they did not build, water from cisterns they did not dig, vineyards and orchards they did not plant—may cause them to forget God (Deut. 6:10–12). Apparently, Satan's hope is that Jesus, blinded by the vision of prosperity, glory, and power, will forget God. As rightful heir to "the throne of his father David" (Luke 1:32), Jesus will ultimately receive more glory and authority than Satan can offer. Yet Jesus' desire is not simply to possess his inheritance, but to receive it as a gift from his Father's hand. Because he loves God with all his heart, he refuses to worship Satan, and he refuses to accept for himself any honor except that which brings glory to God.

Finally, Jesus' victory over temptation in the wilderness confirms that *he trusts God's promises, even when they are not confirmed by outward circumstances.* Two times Satan prefaces his temptations with the phrase, "If you are the Son of God." Satan apparently reasons that Jesus' status should guarantee immunity from suffering; surely God's Son should be full, not hungry, and surely he should enjoy safety, not harm. According to such logic, promises like those of Psalm 91 (from which Satan quotes) should keep Jesus from injury, even if he were to throw himself from "the pinnacle of the temple" (Luke 4:9). Jesus, however, stands firmly on the command of Deuteronomy 6:16: "You shall not put the Lord your God to the test." As the remainder of this verse indicates, the definitive example of "testing" God occurred at Massah, when Israel complained of having no water to drink (Ex. 17:1–7). Despite having their deliverance from Egypt as testimony, the people of Israel allowed the trying circumstances of the wilderness to cast doubt on God's faithful love; in the words of Exodus 17:7, they "tested the Lord by saying, 'Is the Lord among us or not?'"

Satan tempts Jesus with a similar question: "Is God your Father or not?" Jesus, however, doesn't need to prove what has already been promised. At his baptism, God declared, "You are my beloved Son; with you I am well pleased" (Luke 3:22). Unlike Israel, who lived like abandoned orphans despite God's promise that "Israel is my firstborn son" (Ex. 4:22), Jesus honors his Father by resting in what God has declared. Satan tempts Jesus to seek assurance of his Father's love in his outward circumstances; instead, Jesus finds it in his Father's promise.

## Jesus' Passion in the Garden

A third place where Jesus' commitment to God's glory is especially evident is the garden of Gethsemane. Here, having interpreted his coming death at the Last Supper, and anticipating his betrayal and arrest, Jesus offers one of the most profound prayers ever uttered: "Father, if you are willing, remove this cup from me. Nevertheless, not my will, but yours, be done" (Luke 22:42). As simple as it is, this prayer stresses Jesus' devotion to God in three ways.

### *Honoring God through Prayer*

First, Jesus' prayer on the Mount of Olives honors God as a Father who can be trusted to listen lovingly and respond wisely. Elsewhere Jesus has taught others to pray, teaching them to see God as more loving and generous than a human father (Luke 11:11–12), more compassionate than any earthly friend (Luke 11:5–10), more just than any human judge (Luke 18:1–8). Now Jesus honors God through his own prayer, seeking strength from a loving and wise Father during a moment of crisis. Before and after his prayer, Jesus exhorts the apostles to "[p]ray that you may not enter into temptation" (Luke 22:40, 46), suggesting that Jesus is himself seeking strength to obey God's will. In his hour of need—just as he calls his disciples to do—Jesus displays confidence in and reliance on God.

Here we should note that the prayer at Gethsemane represents part of a much larger pattern in Jesus' life. More than any other Gospel writer, Luke emphasizes Jesus' practice of prayer.[3] At Luke 5:16, Luke notes that as Jesus' reputation was growing, "he would withdraw to desolate places and pray"; the context suggests dependence on God for strength, and the grammar indicates that this was Jesus' regular practice. An all-night prayer vigil precedes Jesus' selection of the twelve apostles (Luke 6:12–13), and it is as Jesus is praying that the transfiguration occurs (Luke 9:28–29). According to Luke, it is just after Jesus finishes praying that a disciple says, "Lord, teach us to pray" (Luke 11:1), confirming that we are to learn from Jesus' example. When he hears of the success of the seventy-two missionaries he has sent out, Jesus prays with joyful thanksgiving, honoring God as both "Father" and "Lord of heaven and earth" (Luke 10:21–22), and on three occasions we are told that he gives thanks for food and drink (Luke 9:16; 22:17, 19; 24:30). As we shall see below, Jesus continues to pray even during his crucifixion, confirming that his prayer at Gethsemane is simply one expression—albeit a profound one—of Jesus' dependence on, trust in, and love for God.

### *Honoring God through Submission*

The prayer at Gethsemane also teaches us that Jesus honors God through submission. There is no more profound commentary on the need to submit our desires to God's than the phrase, "not my will, but yours, be done." This prayer confronts us with deep mysteries: How can God's Son request something other than what his Father wills? How could there be tension between the will of Jesus and that of God? The reality of the incarnation

3. For a thorough treatment of the theme, see David M. Crump, *Jesus the Intercessor: Prayer and Christology in Luke-Acts*, Biblical Studies Library (Grand Rapids: Baker, 1999).

points us toward answers. Jesus is preparing to endure betrayal, arrest, and the agonies of the cross not simply as the Son of God, but as the Son of God *who has taken on humanity*, and who must carry out his Father's purposes *as a human being*. Like any other flesh-and-blood human being facing such suffering and sorrow, Jesus would prefer another path; the fact that he *nonetheless* submits to God's will only heightens our appreciation for how deeply he loves his Father.

Again, such submission is characteristic of Jesus' entire life. As we noted earlier, Jesus often speaks of his ministry with phrases like "I must" and "it is necessary," indicating that his life is governed by his Father's purpose. On several occasions he explicitly says that whatever authority he has is not his own, but comes from God: "the one who rejects me rejects him who sent me" (Luke 10:16); "All things have been handed over to me by my Father" (Luke 10:22); "it is by the finger of God that I cast out demons" (Luke 11:20); "I assign to you, as my Father assigned to me, a kingdom" (Luke 22:29). Similarly, Jesus defines his own identity not in terms of human kinship but in terms of obedience to God's commands. His mother and brothers are "those who hear the word of God and do it" (Luke 8:21); blessedness is not available only to Mary, who bore him and nursed him, but to "those who hear the word of God and keep it!" (Luke 11:28). Even when he enters Jerusalem as king, Jesus comes "in the name of the Lord" (Luke 13:35; 19:38). Jesus exercises great authority, but always in a manner which reflects submission to, rather than independence from, God.

### *Honoring God through Suffering*

Finally, Jesus' prayer at Gethsemane expresses his willingness to honor God by enduring great suffering to accomplish God's purpose. Jesus' request is for his Father to "remove this cup from me." Elsewhere in the Gospels, Jesus uses the image of a cup to symbolize suffering (Matt. 20:22–23; Mark 10:38–39; John 18:11). The background for Jesus' image is the Old Testament's comparison of sinners experiencing wrath to people forced to drink from a cup filled with wine until they are drunk, staggering in anguish and misery (see Ps. 75:8; Isa. 51:17, 22; Jer. 25:15; 51:7; Hab. 2:15–16; see also Rev. 14:10; 16:19). It is dread of experiencing such condemnation on our behalf that causes Jesus to ask God to remove the cup, and that leads to the "agony" described in Luke 22:44. But despite knowing that his death would involve draining this cup to its last drop, Jesus still prays, "not my will, but yours, be done." Though it will cost him everything, Jesus' desire to promote God's glory by obeying his purposes makes him willing to endure the greatest suffering imaginable.

## Jesus' Passion on the Cross

While Jesus' passion for God's glory governs his entire life, we have seen it especially clearly in the temple, in the wilderness, and in the garden of Gethsemane. But the final place we must visit to appreciate his devotion to God is the cross. As Jesus willingly goes to his own death, we see the culmination of his obedience to his Father. His loyalty to God's kingdom is such that he is willing to pay any price, even that of his own life. In addition, Jesus' prayers during his crucifixion, and his promise to the repentant criminal crucified alongside him, show us that he continues to trust his Father, even as the circumstances of his own life are at their worst.

Jesus' prayer for the soldiers who nailed him to the cross—"Father, forgive them, for they know not what they do" (Luke 23:34)—is rightly understood to indicate Jesus' compassion on his enemies. Yet it also reveals that Jesus, already hanging on the cross, continues to trust that his Father is full of mercy. This is also true of the last of Jesus' prayers recorded by Luke, a citation from Psalm 31:5: "Father, into your hands I commit my spirit" (Luke 23:46). Despite the fact that he is dying an accursed death, betrayed by his closest followers, mocked by his enemies, and drinking the cup of God's wrath, Jesus continues to think of God as a Father whose hands represent safety. Though he is challenged three times to save himself (Luke 23:35–39), Jesus' attitude remains that of the psalmist: "I trust in you, O Lord; I say, 'You are my God.' My times are in your hand; rescue me from the hand of my enemies and from my persecutors! Make your face shine on your servant; save me in your steadfast love!" (Ps. 31:14–16). Even at the moment of death, Jesus would rather entrust himself to his Father's steadfast love than attempt to deliver himself.

A final indication of Jesus' trust in God is his promise to the criminal who asks to be remembered in Jesus' kingdom: "Truly, I say to you, today you will be with me in Paradise" (Luke 23:43). Together with Luke 24:26 ("Was it not necessary that the Christ should suffer these things and enter into his glory?"), Jesus' words to the criminal indicate that he looks forward to glory when his suffering has ended. God has promised that resurrection and exaltation will follow death and humiliation, that those who weep shall laugh, that the hungry shall feast. Jesus not only communicates such promises to others, he believes them for himself.[4] He need not save himself, nor let suffering cause him to doubt that he is God's "Chosen One" (Luke 23:35), because his Father has promised to deliver him. Even when most around him have concluded that God's promises have failed, Jesus continues to trust the Father.

## Conclusion: A Final Objection?

At this point we must ask whether Jesus' intimate union with his Father is so unique that none of us could hope to

4. Compare Heb. 12:2, which teaches that as Jesus "endured the cross" he was motivated by "the joy that was set before him."

imitate his devotion to God. The testimony of Jesus himself suggests otherwise. He teaches us to pray to God as "Father" (Luke 11:2; see also Luke 11:13), calls us to be merciful because "your Father" is merciful (Luke 6:36), and urges us to trust "your Father" to supply every need (Luke 12:30, 32). Even Luke 10:22, which makes clear the unique connection between God and his Son Jesus, points to the fact that Jesus reveals God to us *as Father*: "no one knows who the Son is except the Father, or who the Father is except the Son *and anyone to whom the Son chooses to reveal him*."

Here, then, is a key distinction. Jesus knows the Father immediately, whereas our knowledge of the Father comes to us through Jesus. Yet it is the Son's mission to enable us to become beloved children of our heavenly Father. As Jesus the unique Son glorifies his Father through love, trust, and obedience, all who follow him are called to do the same. The eternal Son, whose loving obedience secures our place in the Father's family, is also a role model for those of us who are adopted sons and daughters. What would it look like, then, for adopted children to share our older brother's passion for the Father's glory? This is the question we will answer in our next chapter.

# 6

# Imitating Jesus' Passion for the Glory of God

WHEN I WAS IN ELEMENTARY SCHOOL, comic books featured an ad summarizing every boy's greatest fear: a muscular teenager humiliates you, the 98-pound weakling, by kicking sand in your face at the beach in front of all the girls. But never fear—for $2.95 you can order a book from famous muscleman Charles Atlas, whose simple exercises will instantly transform you into a giant! Of course, it's too good to be true, as the book turns out to be just another advertisement. Still, I suspect that most of us have a "Charles Atlas" dream when it comes to imitating Jesus' passion for God's glory. We want a set of simple guidelines that will transform us from spiritual weaklings into giants of faith. And yet we are afraid that when we send in our $2.95, we will get a booklet that tells us to read the Bible and pray and love God—exactly the things we are too weak to do!

There is no set of simple guidelines for loving God's glory as Jesus did, no "get-strong-quick" gimmicks to substitute for a lifetime of walking with our Savior. Still, our progress in imitating Jesus' example can be measured by five practical indicators we will review in this chapter:

- Hating hypocrisy
- Hating idolatry
- Loving God's Word
- Loving God's work
- Loving God's presence

As we cultivate these forms of holy hatred and their corresponding loves, we will grow in Christlike passion for God's glory.

## Imitating Jesus' Passion by Hating Hypocrisy

To most of us, the word *hypocrisy* suggests a blatant contradiction between what someone claims to believe and how he or she actually lives. This often involves pretense—a conscious awareness on one's part that he is merely acting or playing a role. We see this in Luke 20:19–26, where a group of spies asks Jesus a question about paying tribute to Caesar: they pretend (Luke's verb is *hypokrinomai*, related to our term *hypocrite*) to respect Jesus' teaching, but their real intent is to trap him. Yet in most instances in the New Testament, hypocrisy involves a more devastating form of contradiction. When Jesus calls people "hypocrites," he means three things: (1) they are sincerely convinced that their spiritual expertise is advancing God's purposes and helping God's people, (2) they are actually hindering God's purposes and harming God's people, and (3) *the hypocrites themselves are totally oblivious to this contradiction*. On the football field, such hypocrites would not be running trick plays or using deception; instead, they would be oblivious to the fact that they were running the wrong way with the ball, celebrating as each step took them nearer to victory for their opponents. It is no wonder, then, that Jesus hates hypocrisy enough to rail against it, and to warn his disciples to beware its subtle influence (Luke 12:1).

As we grow in likeness to Jesus, we too must develop a hatred for various hypocritical tendencies that distort God's purposes and injure God's people. These include:

- *Selective obedience to Scripture*: We make a mockery of God's Word when we look for ways to "obey" his law while neglecting justice and love (Luke 11:42), failing to extend mercy to those in need (Luke 6:9; 14:3), or shrinking the number of neighbors we must love (Luke 10:29). Christlike love for God involves sensitivity to all the teachings of Scripture, not just those we are comfortable emphasizing.
- *The use of godliness as a means to gain*: Jesus strongly denounces religious leaders who use piety to hide theft (Luke 20:47), greed (Luke 11:39; 16:14–15), and the pursuit of public recognition (Luke 11:43; 20:46–47). Today we might act like generous givers, when in fact we are only interested in tax breaks; or we might promise to pray for friends, hoping they will think we pray more faithfully than in fact we do. But as we are conformed more to Jesus' example, we will become more sensitive to—and quicker to repent of—the use of piety as a mask for selfishness.
- *Eagerness to criticize others, combined with ignorance of our own faults*: Jesus calls the person who can see a speck in another's eye but not the log in his own a "hypocrite" (Luke 6:39–42). A Christlike hatred of such hypocrisy will cause us to ask why we are criticizing others, and whether we are equally rigorous in examining ourselves.

Having identified such tendencies, our sinful temptation will be to condemn others who display them. A more Christlike use of this holy hatred would involve guarding against hypocritical tendencies in our own lives, and extending mercy to others who are being mistreated or misled by hypocrisy.

## Imitating Jesus' Passion by Hating Idolatry

When we consider imitating Jesus' passion for God's glory, we must recognize that our own passion is often misplaced. We orient our lives around things other than God, or around false visions of who he is. To develop a healthy, Christlike love for God therefore requires that we repent of and guard against idolatry.

Though Luke's Gospel never employs the terms *idol* or *idolatry*, Jesus warns against many things that compete for the devotion of our hearts. Here we mention three idols that receive special attention in Luke:

- *Wealth*: "You cannot serve God and money," Jesus bluntly declares (Luke 16:13). Therefore we must "be on . . . guard against all covetousness, for one's life does not consist in the abundance of his possessions" (Luke 12:15). If God is our master and Lord, then retirement accounts, salary packages, homes, cars, and the culture of consumption cannot be. In Luke 18 we see the power of this idol, as love of wealth keeps a rich ruler from following Jesus; in Luke 19, we see the power of the gospel, as the joy of salvation sets Zacchaeus free from bondage to money.
- *Status*: Jesus repeatedly warns against self-exaltation (Luke 14:11; 18:14), prideful disdain of others (Luke 18:9), and the tendency to court favor with those who can bolster our reputation (Luke 14:12–14). The pursuit of recognition from others, or even from God, can easily become an idol that pulls us away from the God who exalts the lowly, and

from the Savior who endures humiliation before he enters his glory.[1]

- *The cares of life*: According to Jesus, the good news of God's Word can be choked out by "the cares and riches and pleasures of life" (Luke 8:14; see also Luke 10:41; 21:34). Even God's good gifts—like fields, oxen, and marriage—can become excuses for avoiding his presence (Luke 14:16–24). We must be on our guard, so that busyness, distractions, and the tyranny of the urgent do not keep us from giving ourselves to God.

When we are growing in Christlike love for God, we will steadfastly resist anything that threatens to diminish his glory or to distract us from his purposes. Like Jesus, we must convince others of the worthlessness of idols; unlike Jesus, we must also repent of our own idolatry, learning to hate our own tendency to serve two masters.

While we can put created things in the place of our Creator, we can also worship false images of that Creator. These, too, are idols which we must learn to hate. Some of us worship a God who can be so impressed with our obedience that he owes us his favor (Luke 17:7–10; 18:9–14); a God who rejoices only in the "righteous . . . who need no repentance," and who would never celebrate the return of a lost son (Luke 15:1–32); or a God whose demands can be softened so that they don't present us with any real challenge (Luke 10:25–37; 18:18–23). But according to Jesus, no such God exists. To worship such a caricature of God is idolatry, and we must develop a holy hatred for worshiping the God of our own imagining.

Put another way, true passion for God's glory involves loving the whole God, the totality of God as he truly is. There is

1. We will examine Luke's emphasis on humiliation and exaltation in greater detail in chapters 9 and 10.

no God who is Father but not King, Savior but not Lawmaker, Redeemer but not Sovereign Creator—no God who is merciful, tender, intimate, to the exclusion of all else. Likewise, there is no God who is King but not Father, Lawmaker but not Savior, Sovereign Creator but not Redeemer—no God who is just, holy, severe, and demanding, to the exclusion of all else. Combining this insight with the biblical command to love God with all of our heart, soul, strength, and mind (Luke 10:27), we may draw an important conclusion: *Christlike passion for the glory of God involves the whole person loving the whole God.* As we follow the example of Jesus, we will grow toward the goal of delighting, with all that we are, in all that God is.

## Imitating Jesus' Passion by Loving God's Word

We've all heard some variation of the joke: the daydreaming Sunday school student has no idea what question the teacher just asked, so he blurts out, "Read the Bible and pray!"—and is congratulated for his response. To say that being like Jesus involves loving God's Word sounds like just such a predictable answer. But as we saw in chapter 5, it is impossible to deny the importance of Scripture in Luke's portrait of Jesus' life. From that portrait, we can derive four principles which should increasingly shape our lives as we imitate Jesus' love of Scripture.

1. *We must sense our absolute need of Scripture for spiritual life and growth.* This is implied by the first words we hear Jesus say. When we first hear from Jesus, he is at the temple, "sitting among the teachers" (Luke 2:46) discussing the meaning of Scripture, and saying to Mary and Joseph, "I must be in my Father's house" (Luke 2:49). The next time we hear from Jesus, he is resisting temptation in the wilderness by citing Scripture to Satan: "Man shall not live by bread alone" (Luke 4:4, citing Deut. 8:3). Just as food is

necessary to sustain physical life, there can be no spiritual life apart from the truth revealed in God's Word. If this was true for Jesus, we can be sure it is true for us as well.

2. *We must seek deep, personal knowledge of Scripture.* Luke's Gospel repeatedly warns us that there can be a superficial, hypocritical knowledge of the Bible; even Satan is familiar enough with the biblical text to recite it accurately (Luke 4:10–11). By contrast, we see that Scripture has deeply penetrated Jesus' heart, flowing from him in moments of intense struggle, emotion, and need. Consider a few examples:

   - Combating Satan's temptations in the wilderness, Jesus turns again and again to Scripture (Luke 4:1–13).
   - Driving merchants from the temple, Jesus explains his action by saying, "It is written, 'My house shall be a house of prayer'" (Luke 19:46, citing Isa. 56:7).
   - Committing his spirit into his Father's hands at the moment of death (Luke 23:46), Jesus recites Psalm 31:5.

   Jesus' knowledge of Scripture calls us not to despair that our love of God's Word is so weak by comparison, but to rejoice that the same Word can feed us deeply and personally as well.

3. *We must develop a holistic, redemptive understanding of Scripture.* Jesus' conflict with other teachers often hinges on their failure to see how specific biblical commands (such as tithing or Sabbath keeping) fit together with other biblical truths (such as justice, mercy, and love). By contrast, Jesus sees that all of Scripture—"the Law of Moses and the Prophets and the Psalms"—works together for one ultimate purpose, which is the worldwide spread of the redemption that God

accomplishes through Jesus (Luke 24:44–47). Our duty to love the Word like Jesus does not mean that we must all become full-time Bible teachers. But it does mean that we are called to love all of its teachings, and to grow in our desire to relate all of its teachings to its ultimate purpose.[2] Jesus' example therefore challenges those of us who love to see the "forest" of Scripture to grow in our appreciation of every "tree," and those of us who know the "trees" intimately to consider the beauty of the "forest."

4. *We learn from Jesus' example the importance of faithful response to the requirements of God's Word.* To "hear the word of God and keep it" is an indicator of nearness to Jesus (Luke 11:28). Therefore, if we love the Word we will obey its commands, knowing that "it is easier for heaven and earth to pass away than for one dot of the Law to become void" (Luke 16:17). But faithful response to Scripture means that we will also cherish its promises, as Jesus cherished the promises of glory after suffering Luke (Luke 24:26), and accept its claims, as Jesus accepted its claims regarding Jonah (Luke 11:29–32) and Moses (Luke 20:37–38). Unlike Jesus, we will not always respond to these requirements as we ought; love for God's Word will then lead us to confess our sin, seeking grace to close the gap between what it requires and how we live.

## Imitating Jesus' Passion by Loving God's Work

Passion for God's glory leads us not only to love his Word, but to love his work—that is, to love doing the things that God calls

2. Practically, three questions (based on the Heidelberg Catechism Q. 2) can help us relate any passage of Scripture to this ultimate purpose: (1) How does this text show us our need of the redemption which God has accomplished through Jesus? (2) How does this text show us God's gracious provision for the redemption of sinners? (3) How does this text call us to respond to God's gracious provision, and thus to participate in the worldwide spread of redemption?

us to do. We certainly see this commitment in Jesus' prayer at Gethsemane, where "Not my will, but yours, be done" (Luke 22:42) is a way of saying, "I love doing what *you* desire more than what *I* desire." Jesus expresses the same commitment at the beginning of his ministry. When crowds urge him to stay in Capernaum, he says, "I *must* preach the good news of the kingdom of God to the other towns as well; for I was sent *for this purpose*" (Luke 4:43).

At this point we might object that Jesus has an unfair advantage over us. For instance, while he can point to Isaiah 61:1 ("[God] has anointed me to proclaim good news to the poor") as proof that he is called to preach, I can't point to a Bible verse that says, "Marry Tricia, have four children, and move to St. Louis to disciple seminary students." How can I love doing God's work like Jesus, when I can't identify that work with the same certainty as Jesus? But this objection fails to distinguish between *mission* and *vocation*. Put simply, mission answers the big-picture question, "What is the overarching goal God wants his people to pursue?," while vocation asks, "What are our individual roles and day-to-day responsibilities in reaching that goal?"[3] For Jesus, mission and vocation overlap in a way that is unique; as a result, it is not appropriate to expect Scripture to spell out the details of my vocation with the same detail that it addresses Jesus' calling as Messiah!

What this means is that *we imitate Christ by furthering his mission, not by duplicating his vocation*. Not all of us are called to be unmarried, itinerant Palestinian rabbis! But each of us does have a part to play in God's mission of extending the blessings of salvation to the ends of the earth (Luke 3:6; 24:47; Acts 1:8; 28:28). As Jesus' ministry makes clear, these blessings include repentance and forgiveness of sins, ongoing maturity as disciples of Jesus

3. Though the term *vocation* is often used as a synonym for *career*, I have in mind here a wider range of issues, including what interests and talents we choose to pursue, whether we marry, child-rearing decisions, and decisions about where to live.

and citizens of God's kingdom, and freedom from suffering in its many forms. In addition, those who experience such blessings should respond with lives marked by two chief characteristics: love for God and love for neighbor. To summarize it in practical terms, then, *we further Christ's mission when, through evangelism, discipleship, and deeds of compassion, we awaken worship of the one true God and multiply mercy to people in need*. But these things can be accomplished through a mind-boggling array of vocations. So my friend who recently took a job as a waitress is not doing "secular" work. She pursues Christlikeness not by praying, "Lord, get me out of this dead-end job so I can really serve you," but by asking, "Father, what are you calling me to do today to awaken others to worship you? Who will I meet today who needs mercy, and how are you calling me to extend it to them?" Whatever our vocation, we can pursue the mission God calls us to with all the zeal that Jesus did.

Two implications follow from our duty to imitate Christ by sharing in his mission of awakening worship and multiplying mercy.

1. *We are called to dedicate our time and energy to serving God, not self.* If we believe that our day-to-day routines have little spiritual significance, we will likely evaluate them in terms of self-fulfillment (does what I do make me feel good about myself?) or self-promotion (does what I do make others feel good about me?). As a result, we will view our vocational choices selfishly, as though they were unrelated to God and his purpose for us: "I will go to this college, because it is prestigious. I will take this job, because it commands a high salary. I will put off marriage so that I can climb the corporate ladder. I will have children one day, but I won't let parenting interfere with my career." But in Jesus we see a passion

for God's purposes that refuses to act independently of God. Instead of living for the next paycheck, the admiration of others, or better self-esteem, a Christlike love of doing God's work leads us to say, "Father, I belong to you. What would you have me do?" Such submission doesn't mean we never have choices to make, but that we view God's agenda, not our own, as primary.

2. *We must combine willingness to bear great cost for God with dependence on him for strength.* To be sure, no person will ever be called to pay a price as high as Jesus did in doing God's work; but extending the blessings of salvation to the ends of the earth demands much sacrifice of every Christian. Clearly, the example of Jesus teaches us that we cannot refuse to bear the cost of such sacrifice. To grow in likeness to him, we must learn to ask constantly, "Father, what costly thing are you calling me to do to awaken worship of you? What costly thing are you calling me to do to multiply your mercy?" Yet Jesus' example also teaches us that we cannot find the strength for such sacrifice within ourselves. At critical moments, Jesus looks outside himself for strength—whether in the wilderness, looking to Scripture rather than to "bread alone" (Luke 4:4); at the Last Supper, anticipating a future day of feasting in a "kingdom" given by his Father (Luke 22:16, 18, 29–30); at Gethsemane, seeking strength through prayer (Luke 22:40–46); or on the cross, trusting his Father for the exaltation that follows humiliation (Luke 23:42–43). Similarly, when the price of doing God's work is greatest, and our circumstances are at their worst, we must seek strength in God's promises and provision. "Father, what gracious thing are you doing to strengthen me to bear this cost?"—this, too, is a question that flows from Christlike love for doing God's work.

## Loving God's Presence

As we have seen to this point, Christlike passion for the glory of God involves growing in our hatred of hypocrisy and idolatry, and in our love for God's Word and God's work. Foundational for all of these, however, is a love for God's presence—a deep sense of intimate union with him that pervades all of life. In Jesus' life, the term that best captures this union is "Father," and the activity that most characteristically expresses it is prayer.

As we saw in chapter 5, even when we take into account his unique status as the Son of God, Jesus' relationship to the Father serves as a pattern for all who are God's "little children" (Luke 10:21). In particular, Luke's Gospel suggests that our relationship with God should reflect the following characteristics of Jesus' interaction with his Father:

1. *We should trust that God is a loving Father who delights to give good gifts to his children.* According to Jesus, since God is a loving Father who knows what his children need, and will give us even his Holy Spirit, we need not be anxious or run after false treasures (Luke 11:11–13; 12:22–34). Jesus too knows what it is to receive good gifts from his Father, whether "a kingdom" (Luke 22:29) or the Spirit (at his baptism, Luke 3:22; after his resurrection, Luke 24:49; Acts 1:4; 2:33).
2. *We should honor and revere our Father as the sovereign king over all creation.* This not only reflects Jesus' prayer at Luke 10:21 ("I thank you, Father, Lord of heaven and earth"), but the opening petitions of the Lord's prayer ("Father, hallowed be your name. Your kingdom come," Luke 11:2). Our nearness to God as Father should not diminish but intensify our desire to exalt, serve, and honor him.
3. *We should rejoice in God's compassion toward the least, lost, and excluded, reflecting his mercy in the way we treat others.*

Jesus sees God as a Father who cares for children who can neither feed themselves (Luke 11:11–12) nor make themselves wise (10:21), and who welcomes into his kingdom little ones who are normally excluded as insignificant (Luke 18:15–17). Like his Father, Jesus rejoices to forgive repentant sinners, and to welcome them while others grumble (Luke 15:1–32). Similarly, Jesus calls us to extend mercy to our enemies for the simple reason that our Father is merciful (Luke 6:27–36).

4. *We should find strength to overcome temptation and trials in our identity as God's children.* On two occasions, God audibly affirms Jesus' identity as his Son (Luke 3:23; 9:35). The first prepares Jesus to encounter temptation in the wilderness ("If you are the Son of God . . .") and rejection at Nazareth ("Is not this Joseph's son?"). The second occurs immediately after Jesus first predicts his coming rejection and death (Luke 9:22, 26). Perhaps it is not surprising, then, that in his prayers at Gethsemane and from the cross, Jesus addresses God as "Father." Similarly, though none of us is the eternal Son of God or his chosen Messiah, God's love for us as his children should strengthen us to resist Satan's lies and to endure the scorn of those who oppose our Father.

By portraying Jesus as the Son of a Father who welcomes many other children into his family, Luke's Gospel suggests that believers are like younger siblings looking up to an older brother. Because Jesus treasures an intimate connection with a glorious Father, we show "family resemblance" when we do the same.

Practically speaking, we see Jesus' enjoyment of God's presence most clearly in his prayer life—a fact emphasized more in Luke than in any other Gospel. But what would it mean to model our praying on that of Jesus? Answers emerge when we observe three trends in Luke's depictions of Jesus at prayer. First, Jesus' example stresses the *practice* of prayer more than its *mechanics*. Luke doesn't comment, for instance, on Jesus' typical posture for prayer (we are told he kneels at Gethsemane, Luke 22:41). On several occasions Jesus withdraws to isolated places for prayer (see Luke 5:16; 6:12; 22:41), though he is often accompanied by at least some of his disciples (Luke 9:18, 28; 11:1). As for the length of Jesus' prayers, we learn that he prays "all night" on one occasion (Luke 6:12), but of four recorded prayers, the longest (Luke 10:21) is only twenty-nine words in Greek! Still, while he draws little attention to the mechanics of Jesus' prayer life, Luke mentions a dozen occasions—from Jesus' baptism to the moment of his death—when Jesus prays or gives thanks. A life modeled on that of Christ will, therefore, demonstrate that the practice of prayer is not optional, even though there is a range of freedom regarding its mechanics; put more simply, Jesus' example allows room for debating *how* (or how long, or how frequently) we should pray, but not *whether* we should pray.

Second, Jesus' example teaches us to make our prayers *wide* and *deep*—that is, expressing a wide variety of *attitudes*, all deeply rooted in a single *conviction*. Depending on his circumstances, Jesus prays with joy (Luke 10:21), thanksgiving (Luke 10:21; 22:17, 19), urgent pleading (Luke 22:32), submission (Luke 22:42), impassioned persistence (Luke 22:44, "more earnestly"), and a trust that combines defiance and desperation (Luke 23:43). Yet on each of the four occasions that Luke records words spoken by Jesus in prayer, Jesus addresses God as "Father" (Luke 10:21; 22:42; 23:34; 23:43). Whatever the circumstances, God is a Father who can be trusted to hear, and to respond in wisdom and love. As we imitate Jesus' example, then, we will not treat prayer as an isolated religious activity, something to be checked off a list of pious works; rather, we will pray because we know that our Father is good, that he is strong, and that he is near.

Finally, Jesus' example teaches us that prayer is especially necessary on certain kinds of *occasions*. For instance, Jesus prays as he transitions to his public ministry (Luke 3:21), as he prepares to choose the twelve apostles (Luke 6:12), both before and after first revealing to the apostles that his mission as Messiah includes his dying and rising (Luke 9:18, 28–29), and at the moment of his death (Luke 23:43). To be sure, each of these events is unique in the history of salvation, and none of them should be reduced to a reminder that we need to pray at our own "key moments." Still, the pattern does suggest that at times of transition when special wisdom and courage are needed, we should seek it from our Father. Similarly, Jesus prays at times of crisis and great difficulty, whether for his disciples when their faith is tested to the point of failing (Luke 22:32), for himself as he wrestles with the cost of doing God's will (Luke 22:42), or for his enemies as they crucify him (Luke 23:34). Again, these prayers represent more than object lessons for our prayer life. Yet they do call us to plead urgently for God to provide strength and mercy at just those moments when we or others are overwhelmed. To imitate Jesus in this is not to make light of his "loud cries and tears" (Heb. 5:7), but to honor him by demonstrating that we, too, trust our Father to give gifts that can come only from him.[4]

## Conclusion: A Final Encouragement

Throughout this chapter, we have examined ways in which we are called to imitate Jesus' passion for the glory of God, whether negatively (hating hypocrisy and idolatry) or positively (loving God's Word, work, and presence). But we are reminded of the limits of imitation by one key difference in our prayer lives—namely, while Jesus teaches us to pray *daily* for the forgiveness

4. For further reflection on what it means to imitate Jesus' passion for God's Word, work, and presence, see Leslie T. Hardin, *The Spirituality of Jesus: Nine Disciplines Christ Modeled for Us* (Grand Rapids: Kregel, 2009).

of our sins (Luke 11:3–4), he never utters such a prayer himself. Our rebellion against God is why we need Jesus to be not just a role model, but a Redeemer. Because we need him to be more than we are, we will not be exactly like him in every respect. But the fact remains that those who are set free *from* sin will, in very significant ways, come to resemble the only person who has ever lived a life completely free *of* sin—Jesus himself.

I find great hope in that truth, especially since writing this chapter has convinced me more than ever that I am, spiritually speaking, a 98-pound weakling. Gazing at the glories of Christ's life, I feel the coldness of my own love for God, the weakness of my prayers, the hardness of my heart toward my Father. But when I truly focus on Jesus, and not on myself, I see that God doesn't call me to become a Charles Atlas muscleman, able to vanquish bullies in my own strength. Instead, while I am weak, he sends a Savior to conquer my enemies! When we grasp this truth, our weakness serves not as a barrier to our passion for God's glory, but as an invitation to delight again in how great his glories are.

# 7

# Jesus' Passion for the Good of Others

IN A 1941 ARTICLE, Mahatma Gandhi had the following to say about Jesus:

> [H]e was certainly the highest example of one who wished to give everything, asking nothing in return, and not caring what creed might happen to be professed by the recipient. I am sure that if he were living here now among men, he would bless the lives of many who perhaps have never even heard of his name, if only their lives embodied the virtues of which he was a living example on earth; the virtues of loving one's neighbour as oneself and of doing good and charitable works among one's fellowmen.[1]

Gandhi's words represent a common contemporary view of Jesus: he was a great example of love, kindness, and compassion, who cared little for doctrine or for whether people made a religious

1. Mahatma Gandhi, "What Jesus Means to Me," Sacredliving.org, http://www.sacred-living.org/gandhi-what-Jesus-means-to-me (accessed January 23, 2012). The article was originally published in 1941 in the Indian magazine *The Modern Review.*

commitment to him. Yet such a view cannot possibly emerge from a detailed reading of the Gospels, where Jesus' deeds of love, kindness, and compassion are interwoven with particular doctrinal claims (about himself, God, and Scripture, among other things) and demands for exclusive allegiance to him. Instead, this view of Jesus is founded on a vague sense that Jesus "did good things" and wanted other people to "do good things" too.

In this chapter, we seek to discover how Jesus devotes himself to benefiting, blessing, and doing good to other people. But in order to build our understanding of Jesus' example on a solid foundation, we must carefully observe the patterns of Jesus' life and ministry as they are depicted in Scripture. Therefore, this chapter will focus on one main question: in Luke's Gospel, how does Jesus demonstrate passion for the good of others? As we look to the details of the biblical text, we will discover a paradox that Gandhi failed to grasp: only when we see Jesus as *more* than a role model of virtue will we feel the full force of his example.

## Three Reasons to Look to Jesus' Example

As already noted, it doesn't take much to persuade people today, whether they are Christians or not, that Jesus is a good role model of love, kindness, and compassion. But before moving ahead in this chapter, it is worth asking whether Luke intends us to view Jesus in this way. Three features of Luke's Gospel combine to answer this question with a resounding, "Yes!"

### *Jesus' Teaching*

Jesus' teaching sets a premium on love for our fellow human beings. Early in Luke's Gospel he calls us to treat others as we wish to be treated (Luke 6:31). Soon after, he confirms that the duty to love "your neighbor as yourself" (Luke 10:27) is second only to love for God. According to Jesus, the demands of such neighbor love are extreme: our "neighbor" includes anyone in need of mercy, no matter how despised (Luke 10:25–37); we are even to love our enemies, just as God is "kind to the ungrateful and the evil" (Luke 6:27–36). But if Jesus demands this kind of love from his disciples, we may expect him also to model it, because he is a trustworthy teacher, and not a "blind guide."

### *Jesus' Embodiment of God's Mercy*

A second indication that we are to follow Jesus' example of love for others is found in Luke 6:36, "Be merciful, even as your Father is merciful." According to Jesus, God's mercy to us provides a pattern for us to imitate. Yet throughout Luke's Gospel, it is *Jesus* who embodies God's mercy. This is especially clear when we observe the correspondence between how Jesus acts and what he teaches about God. The following texts illustrate the pattern:

- In the parable of the moneylender (Luke 7:41–43), it is God who forgives debtors, but it is Jesus who goes on to declare a sinful woman forgiven (Luke 7:44–50).
- In the parable of the great banquet (Luke 14:16–24), it is God who invites "the poor and crippled and blind and lame" to feast, yet it is Jesus who has just criticized a prominent Pharisee for failing to invite "the poor, the crippled, the lame, [and] the blind" to his own meals (Luke 14:12–14).
- In the parables of Luke 15, it is God the Father who celebrates when lost sinners are found, while it is Jesus' association with tax collectors and sinners that prompts the telling of the parables (Luke 15:1–32).

The implication is clear: we heed Jesus' call to imitate God's mercy by conforming to the example of Jesus, who embodies that mercy.

### *Jesus versus False Leaders*

As is the case with passion for the glory of God (see chapter 5), Luke's Gospel depicts Jesus as a model of passion for the good of others by contrasting him with false leaders. He is not like the Pharisees and scribes, who "neglect justice and the love of God"[2] (Luke 11:42) and whose teaching wearies, burdens, and hinders those who hear it (Luke 11:46, 52). Jesus extends mercy to sinners while these religious leaders grumble (Luke 5:30; 7:34, 39; 15:2), and he heals when they demonstrate more concern for livestock than for human misery (Luke 13:10–17; 14:1–6). Jesus must even rebuke his own disciples for threatening vengeance (Luke 9:54; 22:49–50) and for showing disdain for outsiders (Luke 9:49) and children (Luke 18:15–17). Through such contrasts, Luke's Gospel invites us to embrace Jesus as the paradigm of proper concern for others.

## Three Themes from Luke's Gospel: Saving, Seeking, Calling

We will organize the remainder of this chapter around the key themes of *saving*, *seeking*, and *calling*. These are derived from terms Jesus uses to describe his ministry:

- *Luke 19:10*: "For the Son of Man came to seek and to save the lost."
- *Luke 5:32*: "I have not come to call the righteous but sinners to repentance."

This strategy raises challenging questions that we will address in chapter 8: To what extent are Jesus' ministries of seeking, saving, and calling unique? Is it possible, or proper, for Christians

2. That is, "the kind of love demanded by God" (I. Howard Marshall, *The Gospel of Luke: A Commentary on the Greek Text*, New International Greek Testament Commentary [Exeter: Paternoster and Grand Rapids: Eerdmans, 1978], 498).

to imitate Jesus' work of saving the lost? Do some Christians, such as pastors and missionaries, have a greater responsibility for ministries of "seeking" and "calling"? For now, however, we recognize that our strategy yields a significant benefit—namely, it helps us to study Jesus' passion for others' good *using themes that are integral to Luke's Gospel.* As we do so, we will discover that Jesus is first and foremost the Savior who passionately pursues those who are in need of mercy. Yet his redeeming love is also an example for everyone he has saved, sought, and called.

## Jesus' Passion for Saving Others

The vocabulary of salvation appears more often in Luke than in any other Gospel.[3] This vocabulary implies that human beings face a dire threat from which we cannot deliver ourselves—namely, sin and all its consequences, which include God's righteous anger against our disobedience, together with all the spiritual and physical miseries that afflict us and our world. The good news of the gospel is that Jesus is a Savior committed to securing the good of needy people who have no hope apart from him. Because this theme is so prominent in Luke, we will use only a few key texts to demonstrate its various aspects.

### *Jesus Saves Others from Sin*

The early chapters of Luke make it clear that Jesus has come to bless people with salvation (see Luke 1:69, 71; 2:11, 30; 3:6), which includes the forgiveness of sins (Luke 1:76–77). Yet the first time we see this aspect of Jesus' ministry, it takes a somewhat unexpected form: instead of healing a paralyzed man who is brought before him, Jesus first says to him, "Man, your sins are forgiven you" (Luke 5:17–20). Since the critics in the crowd now

3. Luke's Gospel uses the "savior/save/salvation" word group twenty-five times, compared to sixteen in Matthew, fifteen in Mark, and eight in John.

suspect him of blasphemy, Jesus uses a healing miracle to prove that he has "authority on earth to forgive sins" (Luke 5:24). While the text emphasizes Jesus' unique authority, it also reminds us that Jesus is concerned to deliver people from various forms of misery, including God's judgment against our sin.

An episode from Luke 7 confirms that we should see Jesus' forgiveness of sins as an expression of his love for those in need. At the home of Simon the Pharisee, Jesus offends his host by allowing a woman known to be a "sinner" (Luke 7:37) to anoint his feet at a meal. After a short parable that leads Simon to acknowledge that forgiveness of a great debt should prompt great love (Luke 7:41–43), Jesus commends the woman: while Simon has failed to show Jesus any special courtesy, she has shown extraordinary love. Jesus' logic presupposes that forgiveness is an extravagant expression of kindness, since only such a gift could prompt the woman's response. When Jesus forgives sins, he is exercising unique, divine authority. But he is also demonstrating extravagant kindness to those who need mercy.

### *Jesus Saves Others from Sickness*

In Luke's Gospel (and in Scripture as a whole), the concept of salvation is broader than many of us typically imagine. Thus we may be surprised to learn that Jesus says "Your faith has *saved* you" not only to repentant sinners (see Luke 7:50) but also to those healed of physical ailments (Luke 8:48; 17:19; 18:42).[4] In this section, we consider three texts that not only illustrate Jesus' passion for blessing others by saving them from sickness, but suggest that his followers should share this passion as well.

In Luke 6:6–11, Jesus heals a man with a crippled hand while teaching at a synagogue. Because the text involves Jesus' unique

4. This does not mean that it is wrong for translations like the ESV to employ the phrase "Your faith has *made you well*" when physical healing is in view; to be saved from illness is to be made well.

authority over the Sabbath (see Luke 6:5), we cannot treat it as a simple object lesson in compassion for the disabled. Yet the entire narrative is driven by Jesus' insistence that the man be healed without delay, implying that if Jesus' critics truly understood God's law they would be just as zealous to "do good" and to "save life" as Jesus is. A similar message is sent in Luke 7:21–23, when Jesus replies to messengers from John the Baptist who ask if Jesus is the Messiah:

> In that very hour he healed many people of diseases and illnesses and evil spirits, and to many blind people he gave sight. And answering he said to them, "Go report to John the things you saw and heard: blind people are receiving sight, lame people are walking, lepers are being cleansed and deaf people are hearing; dead people are being raised, poor people are having good news preached to them. And blessed is he who is not offended by me." (translation my own)

John is likely puzzled that Jesus' ministry focuses more on mercy to the needy than on powerful acts of judgment against God's enemies. But instead of taking offense, anyone who recognizes Jesus as Messiah should rejoice that he comes to heal, restore, and bless. Taken together, these two texts indicate that even though Jesus' authority is unique, all who embrace him as God's chosen Savior should share his passion for relieving the misery of those devastated by the effects of sin.

Jesus' commitment to bless others is again emphasized when he heals a blind man (called Bartimaeus in Mark 10:46) who twice cries out, "Son of David, have mercy on me!" (Luke 18:38, 39). Jesus then asks a question ("What do you want me to do for you?," Luke 18:41) that interprets the miracle as an act done for the benefit of the blind man. The Son of David not only has power, but passion, to extend mercy to those in need. The contrast between Jesus' readiness to heal and the annoyed attempt of others to silence the blind man (Luke 18:39) again suggests that this passion should be shared by those who rightly understand his merciful character.

### *Jesus Saves Others from Satan*

In addition to saving others from sin and sickness, Jesus delivers people from the power of Satan and evil spirits. Luke often highlights Jesus' mercy for those under demonic influence by detailing their desperate condition. Consider the following texts:

- In Luke 8:26–35, Jesus encounters a man who "for a long time" has lived naked and alone among tombs, overpowered "many a time" by a demon, and ultimately possessed by "many demons." Once Jesus expels the demons, the formerly hopeless man sits at Jesus' feet, "clothed and in his right mind."
- In Luke 9:37–42, a father asks Jesus to help his only son, who is frequently seized by a spirit that violently shakes him until he "foams at the mouth," leaving the boy "shatter[ed]." Though Jesus' disciples have been unable to drive out the demon, Jesus heals the boy and restores him to his father.
- In Luke 13:10–17, Jesus heals a woman who has been crippled by a "disabling spirit" for eighteen years. Despite the protests of a synagogue official, Jesus insists that it is necessary for "this woman . . . whom Satan bound for eighteen years, [to] be loosed from this bond on the Sabbath day."

Such texts certainly emphasize Jesus' unique authority as Messiah; he is able to do what mere humans cannot. Yet they also remind us that Jesus desires—urgently, according to the last text—to see God's enemies defeated, and human beings set free from the miseries they cause.

Finally, Jesus' commitment to delivering others from Satan is evident in words he addresses to Peter following the Last Supper: "Simon, Simon, behold, Satan demanded to have *you*, that he might sift *you* as wheat, but I have prayed for you that your faith may not fail. And when you have turned again, strengthen your brothers" (Luke 22:31–32, italics added to indicate plural pronouns). Through Jesus' arrest and crucifixion, Satan seeks to crush the faith of the apostles as a group ("you" plural). Jesus responds by asking his Father to strengthen Peter's faith ("you/your" singular). Perhaps we are to infer that Jesus prayed similarly for the other apostles, or perhaps Jesus extends his care to them simply through Peter's leadership. Either way, the text demonstrates Jesus' mercy toward those who need protection from Satan's schemes.

### *Jesus Saves Others from Sorrow*

As many of us know too well, it is not without reason that Scripture calls death the "last enemy" (1 Cor. 15:26), capable of causing "sorrow upon sorrow" (Phil. 2:27). We rejoice to know, then, that Jesus demonstrates his passion for others' good by overturning death and the sorrow it brings.

We first witness this aspect of Jesus' ministry as he draws near to the town of Nain and sees a dead man "being carried out, the only son of his mother, and she was a widow, and a considerable crowd from the town was with her. And when the Lord saw her, he had compassion on her and said to her, 'Do not weep'" (Luke 7:12–13). Without doubt, Jesus' ability to restore this man's life with a simple command emphasizes his divine power. Yet Luke tells the story in such a way that our hearts break as we realize the depth of the widow's sorrow. Because Jesus takes action to reverse such grief, the text emphasizes not only his power but his compassion.

In Luke 8:40–56, Jesus confronts two kinds of sorrow. First, he comforts those who feel the pain of death. When he first learns that the only daughter of Jairus, a synagogue leader, has died, he says, "Do not fear; only believe, and she will be well" (Luke 8:50). Later, he says to those at Jairus's house, "Do not weep, for she is not dead but sleeping" (Luke 8:52). Jesus demonstrates his power by restoring the child's life through a simple command; yet he does so in a way that brings comfort to others. Second, Jesus confronts the loneliness that results from being cut off from full fellowship with our neighbors. On the way to Jairus's house, Jesus is touched by a woman who for twelve years has had "a discharge of blood" (Luke 8:43). Though Jesus' power has healed her body, a problem remains: for over a decade the woman's bleeding has made her ceremonially unclean (see Lev. 15:25) and therefore cut off from normal contact with her fellow Israelites. But rather than scolding her for touching him while unclean, Jesus assures the woman that her place in the people of God has been fully restored: "Daughter, your faith has made you well [or, *saved you*]; go in peace" (Luke 8:48). To those afflicted by sorrow, Jesus extends healing, comfort, and peace.

## Jesus' Passion for Seeking Others

At Zacchaeus's house, Jesus announces that he has come "to seek and to save the lost" (Luke 19:10). Like his heavenly Father in Luke 15, Jesus seeks out, gladly welcomes, and celebrates over people of whom many are tempted to say, "Good riddance!" As we shall now see, Luke's Gospel emphasizes Jesus' passionate seeking for two kinds of people in particular.

### *Jesus Seeks the Lost*

In Luke, "the lost" are people who live flagrantly immoral lifestyles and are therefore assumed by many to be beyond the reach of God's mercy. When Jesus seeks such sinners, he sends two messages: first, through faith and repentance anyone, no matter how scandalous their sin, can become a full member of God's family; therefore, second, the common assumption that the lost cannot be redeemed is utterly false. We see both of these themes in Jesus' encounter with Zacchaeus. By working as a tax collector for the hated Romans, Zacchaeus has in effect declared that money means more to him than faithfulness to the God of Israel; thus the crowd is offended that Jesus would go to his house (Luke 19:7). Yet when Zacchaeus repents, Jesus proclaims him a "son of Abraham" (Luke 19:9)! While others are happy to keep sinners outside the boundaries of God's saving love, Jesus offers them a place at the heart of God's purposes.

Such patterns characterize Jesus' entire ministry. In his first sermon he enrages his hearers by reminding them that Elijah and Elisha extended mercy to Gentiles (Luke 4:25–29). Later Jesus praises the faith of "a woman of the city, who was a sinner" (Luke 7:37), while he asserts that Simon the Pharisee is guilty of sin, and has not been forgiven (Luke 7:40–47). In fact, when Jesus is criticized as "a friend of tax collectors and sinners" (Luke 7:34; compare 5:27–30), he appears to be encouraged rather than insulted! Rather than joining with others who deride and condemn the lost, Jesus actively seeks them, even when it means exposing himself to criticism.

### *Jesus Seeks the Least*

If the "lost" are sinners, the "least" are inferiors, people viewed as insignificant in God's purposes and in human society. But Jesus is happy to affirm that those who are least in this world's eyes have significance in God's kingdom, and his ministry is characterized by the welcome acceptance of outsiders.

We first encounter Jesus' heart for the least in his sermon at Nazareth, when he announces that God has anointed him "to proclaim good news to the poor" (Luke 4:18). Joel Green reminds us that in Jesus' day the term *poor* signaled a person's status in the community, which was influenced not only by material wealth but by factors such as "education, gender, family heritage," and so on.[5] The term therefore included all who were on the fringes of human society, often mistreated by their neighbors, and viewed as cursed by God. Yet, as Luke's Beatitudes remind us, Jesus sees the poor, the hungry, the mournful, and the persecuted as the true heirs of God's *blessings* (Luke 6:20–23). Jesus' vision is for an inside-out kingdom in which the status poor can become first, while those who treasure status most will be last (Luke 13:30).

Luke 14:1–14 illustrates Jesus' passion for extending blessing to the least. Dining in the home of a "ruler of the Pharisees" (Luke 14:1), Jesus sees a man with "dropsy" (Luke 14:2), a condition that causes noticeable swelling due to the retention of water. By healing the man, Jesus publicly identifies with an outsider whose body is crippled, rather than with the status-rich "lawyers and Pharisees" who object to Jesus' deed (Luke 14:3). Later, Jesus observes that his socially prominent host has invited only his "friends . . . brothers . . . relatives [and] rich neighbors" (Luke 14:12). Jesus challenges the man instead to "invite the poor, the crippled, the lame, the blind, and you will be blessed" (Luke 14:13–14). Jesus' logic is simple: because God invites outsiders to feast in his kingdom (see the parable of the great banquet in Luke 14:16–24), it is better to be counted among the outsiders, extending blessing to the needy, weak, and status poor.

As is evident by now, Jesus' commitment to seeking the least reverses insider-outsider distinctions that are based on ungodly priorities. Consider three further examples:

- *Jesus honors children*. In Jesus' day, children were viewed as insignificant, only slightly above slaves in terms of social

5. Joel B. Green, *The Gospel of Luke*, The New International Commentary on the New Testament (Grand Rapids and Cambridge: Eerdmans, 1997), 211.

status. Yet Jesus closely identifies himself with a child (Luke 9:46), rebukes his disciples for keeping children from him (Luke 18:15–16), and affirms that God's kingdom belongs "to such" (Luke 18:16).

- *He affirms women.* While women were typically excluded from relationships with rabbis, Jesus commends Mary for her devotion to his teaching (Luke 10:38–42) and includes women among his disciples (see especially Luke 8:1–3). In Jesus' eyes, even the miniscule offering of a poor widow has tremendous spiritual significance (Luke 21:1–4).
- *He commends hated Samaritans.* Though they were viewed as the impure remnant of the idolatrous Northern Kingdom, Jesus portrays the "good Samaritan" in a more positive light than Jewish leaders (Luke 10:29–37), and he commends the faith of a Samaritan leper (Luke 17:11–19).

Since he spends his first night in a manger and dies on a cross, perhaps we should not be surprised that Jesus' passion for seeking the least involves honoring those who are normally despised or neglected.

## Jesus' Passion for Calling Others

On Sunday, September 16, 2001—the first Sunday after the terrorist attacks of 9/11—I was prepared to preach. I had planned for months to use Luke 13:1–9 as my text, and was encouraged by the elders of the church to go ahead, though the imagery of Luke 13:1–5 was especially painful on that morning:

> There were some present at that very time who told [Jesus] about the Galileans whose blood Pilate had mingled with their sacrifices. And he answered them, "Do you think that these Galileans

> were worse sinners than all the other Galileans, because they suffered in this way? No, I tell you; but unless you repent, you will all likewise perish. Or those eighteen on whom the tower in Siloam fell and killed them: do you think that they were worse offenders than all the others who lived in Jerusalem? No, I tell you; but unless you repent, you will all likewise perish."

It is loving to warn people who are in the path of disaster that they need to seek safety; in fact, it would be unloving to fail to issue such a warning, or to issue it with anything less than complete urgency. Here, then, we briefly consider how Jesus demonstrates passion for others' good by calling them to repent.

Throughout his ministry, Jesus calls those who have turned aside from God and his purposes to repentance—but nowhere more memorably than in the parable of the prodigal son (Luke 15:11–32). Through his portrait of the younger brother, Jesus calls sinners who have turned their backs on God to recognize their spiritual bankruptcy and cast themselves on God's mercy (Luke 15:11–24). Similarly, Jesus addresses those guilty of self-righteousness through the older brother (Luke 15:25–32), whose refusal to join the banquet honoring the prodigal symbolizes a refusal to rejoice in God's mercy. Yet Jesus' parable is open-ended; we are not told how the older brother responds when the father leaves the banquet to plead with him for a change of heart (Luke 15:28–32). Even when their sin would seem too great, or their hearts too hard, for reconciliation with God to be possible, Jesus extends love to others by calling them to repent.

Jesus' compassion for unrepentant people is evident in a series of texts concerning Jerusalem and its inhabitants. Though Israel (represented by its capital city) rejects and murders God's messengers, Jesus cries out, "O Jerusalem, Jerusalem . . . ! How often would I have gathered your children together as a hen gathers her brood under her wings, and you were not willing!" (Luke 13:34). The tender imagery confirms that it is Israel who has hardened her heart toward Jesus, not vice-versa. Similarly, as Jesus enters Jerusalem, he not only predicts that God's judgment will result in the city's destruction, but weeps over the fate of those who do not receive him (Luke 19:41–44). Most poignantly, Jesus says to the women following him to Golgotha, "Daughters of Jerusalem, do not weep for me, but weep for yourselves and for your children" (Luke 23:28). Jesus' words to these women about their approaching judgment (Luke 23:29–31) indicate that he has the tragic fate of unrepentant sinners in mind even as his own crucifixion draws near. As he directly confronts those who refuse to repent, Jesus neither forgets their fate nor hardens his heart toward them.[6]

Finally, Jesus loves his own followers by calling them to turn away from anything that would hinder their faithfulness. In the case of Martha (Luke 10:38–42), the hindrance—preparing a meal for Jesus and his companions—seems positive. But Jesus makes it clear that her priorities are misdirected: "Martha, Martha, you are anxious and troubled about many things, but one thing is necessary" (Luke 10:41–42). Note that Jesus' commitment to Martha's good takes an unexpected form: Martha wants mercy in the form of someone to help her with domestic duties; instead, Jesus calls her to break free from her anxiety and devote herself to his teaching. Similarly, at Luke 21:34–36, Jesus warns his followers to "stay awake at all times" as they await his return, lest their hearts be weighed down by sin and anxiety. Though sleepy people want nothing more than to be left alone, Jesus sounds an alarm to rouse them from spiritual drowsiness. Even when they would prefer a more soothing—and dangerous—form of "mercy," Jesus remains committed to others' good.

6. Taken together with the parable of the fig tree (Luke 13:6–9), these texts may also indicate Jesus' hope that warnings will prompt stubborn hearts to change before it is too late.

## Jesus' Death: The Ultimate Display of Passion for Others' Good

Throughout Luke's Gospel we see that Jesus is willing to endure rejection, ridicule, and rage to extend the blessings of salvation to others. As his ministry comes to a close, we discover that Jesus is even prepared to lay down his life for the good of others. Two caveats are in order. First, Luke views Jesus' death as far more than an example of self-sacrificial love. In a way that no other human death can, Jesus' crucifixion accomplishes God's purpose to save sinners. Second, neither Luke's Gospel nor Acts suggests that martyrdom is the only faithful response to the good news about Jesus. Rather, as the ultimate expression of love, Jesus' death calls us to imitate him by doing what is best for others, even at great cost to ourselves. In some circumstances, for some Christians, this will mean literally dying for another's good; in all circumstances, for all Christians, it means putting the interests of our neighbors ahead of our own.

This interpretation of Jesus' death is especially clear in Luke 22. Stressing his self-sacrifice on behalf of others, Jesus declares at the Last Supper, "This is *my body* which is *given for you*. . . . This cup that is *poured out for you* is the new covenant in *my blood*" (Luke 22:19–20). Because his death uniquely seals a "new covenant" of forgiveness (see Jer. 31:31–34), Jesus is more than a role model. Yet, just a few verses later, Jesus reminds the disciples that he is the pattern for their life together. While they have been arguing over who should be "regarded as the greatest," Jesus' status is that of the lowly servant instead of the master: "For who is the greater, one who reclines at table or one who serves? Is it not the one who reclines at table? But I am among you as the one who serves" (Luke 22:24–27). While we will examine this text in detail in chapter 9, we note here a key contrast: as the disciples focus on promoting themselves in order to *receive* recognition *from* others, Jesus is preparing to sacrifice himself in order to *secure* blessing *for* others. While many events in Luke's Gospel demonstrate Jesus' passion for others' good, none does so more powerfully than his crucifixion, where Jesus gives his body and pours out his blood *for us*. In doing so, he is both our Savior and our ultimate example.

## Conclusion: Finding Courage in the Cross

Some readers might be reluctant to turn the page at this point. The pattern of this book is to look at some aspect of Jesus' character and conduct in one chapter, and to ask in the next, "What would it look like to reflect this in our lives?" After seeing the many ways that Jesus seeks the good of other people, all culminating in the sacrifice of his own life, we might not want to answer that question. "Jesus was nice, so I should be nice" sounds a lot safer. But our fears are eased when we realize that the life which stands *before* us as an example, is the same life that was given *for* us at the cross. Whatever Jesus may call us to do for others, he has done infinitely more for us. This truth is a source of joy and strength as we turn the page, asking how we might live for the good of others as he did.

# 8

# Imitating Jesus' Passion for the Good of Others

NEAR MY HOME the Missouri River is spanned by a bridge that includes a bicycle path. A narrow strip of concrete carries cyclists between two dangers—eight lanes of sixty-mile-per-hour traffic on one side, and a fifty-foot plunge into the river on the other. But despite these dangers, scores of riders cross the bridge every day, kept safe by eight-foot fences of concrete and chain link on either side of the bike lane. In this chapter, we find ourselves on a path that Jesus has traveled, a path of passionate devotion to the good of other people. We long to follow where he has led, and to discover what it would look like for us to imitate his example. But following this path will carry us between two dangers: on the one hand, we can so emphasize our duty to imitate Jesus' love for others that we undermine his uniqueness as our Savior; on the other, we can so guard Jesus' unique, saving work that we fail to take seriously our duty to follow his example. Therefore, while the bulk of this chapter will address three marks of Christlike commitment to others' good, we begin by recognizing a series of important scriptural safeguards that form "fences" to protect us as we travel the path our Savior has marked out for us.

## The First Fence: Safeguarding Jesus' Uniqueness

Jesus' miracles are a key expression of his love for others. As we seek to imitate this love, it is therefore important that we safeguard his uniqueness by rightly interpreting his miracles. Three principles help us in this regard:

1. *We must not reduce Jesus' miracles to object lessons in kindness for those in need.* Luke's accounts of Jesus' healing miracles and exorcisms always involve themes that apply uniquely to him, such as the need for faith in him (Luke 8:48, 50), his authority to forgive sins (Luke 5:20–24), his authority to interpret the will of God for the Sabbath (Luke 6:5–11), the legitimacy of his claims over against those of false leaders (Luke 13:10–17), or his power over death, disease, and demons. While it is legitimate to stress the exemplary aspect of Jesus' miracles, such stress must not come at the expense of these other themes.

2. *We must not neglect faith, joy, and worship when drawing applications from Jesus' miracles.* When we read of Jesus' compassion for the widow at Nain (Luke 7:11–17), it is proper to ask how we should care for widows and others in need, or what we might do to comfort those who mourn. However, such questions ought to accompany other applications, such as believing that Jesus has a heart of compassion, expressed through the particular historical act of raising this widow's son; rejoicing that Jesus has authority as Messiah to bring the life-giving blessings of God's kingdom to fulfillment on earth; and praising God for sending Jesus as our Redeemer. The proper response to Jesus' miracles includes both Christ-like compassion and Christ-honoring faith.

3. *We must not confuse the offices of the church when drawing applications from Jesus' miracles.* For our purposes,

it is helpful to distinguish four offices: the unique office of Messiah, held only by Jesus; the transitional office of apostle, held only by a limited number of first-generation Christian leaders; the ongoing "special office" of pastor; and the ongoing "general office" of every Christian believer.[1] When we consider the theme of extending mercy to those in need, we see that there is both continuity and discontinuity among these offices:

- As Messiah, Jesus is uniquely anointed to proclaim "good news to the poor" (Luke 4:18), and he has divine, miraculous power to heal any affliction.
- The apostles are granted authority to heal in Jesus' name (Luke 9:1; 10:9), and they organize church life in such a way that the needs of the poor are not neglected (Acts 4:34–35; 6:1–6).
- As pastors perform their "special office," they have a duty to call the church to care for those in need, and they have a particular responsibility to extend spiritual (and in conjunction with deacons, material) care to those who are in distress.
- Yet all believers have a duty to show mercy to neighbors in need, as the parable of the good Samaritan (Luke 10:25–37) makes especially clear.

Because there is continuity among the offices of the church, it is right to imitate Christ's mercy to those in need. But because the offices are distinct, it is not proper to assume that all Christians should have Jesus' power, the apostles' authority, or a pastor's duties.

1. Compare Edmund P. Clowney, *The Church*, Contours of Christian Theology (Downers Grove, IL: InterVarsity Press, 1995), 207–14.

## The Second Fence: Safeguarding Our Duty

With the preceding principles in place to safeguard Jesus' uniqueness, we may now state four key principles that more positively set forth our duty to imitate his care for those in need. Each derives from my own reflection on how it is proper for Christians to imitate one who is simultaneously our Savior and our example.

1. *It is proper to imitate Christ by extending the kingdom over which he alone reigns.* Jesus is the Son of David, the royal Messiah who brings the blessings of God's kingdom to earth. The Old Testament leads us to expect that where David's greater Son reigns, justice, mercy, and relief from oppression will abound.[2] We imitate Christ not by seeking to reproduce the powerful acts by which he established his reign, but by extending to more and more people the law of love which is at the heart of his kingdom.

2. *It is proper to imitate Christ by inviting others to receive gifts which he alone can give.* Throughout his earthly ministry, Jesus blesses others by calling them to repent and by forgiving their sin. Before his ascension, he commissions the church to carry the message of "repentance and forgiveness of sins . . . to all nations" (Luke 24:47). Yet Acts 5:31 makes it clear that these remain gifts which Jesus alone can bestow, describing him as the one who "give[s] repentance . . . and forgiveness of sins" to God's people. We become imitators of Christ not by claiming authority to forgive sins, but by inviting others to turn from sin and to his mercy, and so receive the gifts which he graciously gives.

2. See Deut. 17:14–20; 2 Sam. 23:3–5; Isa. 9:1–7; Ezek. 34:1–31; and especially Ps. 72.

3. *It is proper to imitate Christ by combating powers that he alone can conquer.* I remember well visiting a terminally ill woman to prepare for her funeral. As I dressed that morning, I had the sense that I was a warrior putting on armor, preparing to do battle with death. Because I was armed with promises founded on Christ's redeeming work, anxiety and despair were pushed back that day. But the fact remains that you and I are powerless against death, disease, and the devil—enemies only Jesus can ultimately conquer. Our calling, then, is not to defeat these enemies, but to continue the fight. And so we comfort those who are facing death, we seek to relieve the misery of those who are diseased or disabled, and we engage (through means summarized in Eph. 6:10–18) in a spiritual struggle against Satan and his allies. Though we cannot duplicate Jesus' power, we can imitate his zeal as we do battle for others' good.

4. *It is proper to imitate Christ by doing extensively what he does intensively.* Unlike other miracles in Luke's Gospel, the feeding of the five thousand (Luke 9:10–17) could have been achieved by human effort. As the apostles suggest (Luke 9:12), the crowd could have dispersed to find food in local villages; or, with sufficient money, the apostles could have purchased food (Luke 9:13). Jesus' divine power enables him to do almost instantly and effortlessly (intensively) what would ordinarily come about only through much time, labor, and resources (extensively). Our inability to duplicate the miraculous means Jesus employed does not mean that we have no duty to imitate his passion for the good of others; rather, we are called to pursue passionately his goals of doing good and saving life (Luke 6:9) through ordinary means.

## Identifying the Marks of Christlike Passion for the Good of Others

In chapter 4 we used the image of a compass to indicate that we would be focusing on four major directions that should govern the Christlike life. In this chapter, we are following one of those directions in particular. But as anyone who has used a compass to navigate unfamiliar terrain can attest, after choosing a heading you must also identify distinctive landmarks—such as trees, fence posts, or boulders—lying along that heading. These are used to confirm that you are remaining on course, not drifting from the desired direction as you travel. Similarly, having chosen the heading of Christlike passion for the good of others, and having outlined principles that can help to keep us on the path, we now identify three distinctive markers that indicate progress toward our goal.

### *The First Mark: Hospitality*

Luke's Gospel emphasizes the fact that *Christlike passion for the good of others expresses itself in hospitality*. Initially, this may sound strange to us. After all, Jesus had no home in which to entertain guests, he was fed by others far more often than he fed them, and only at the Last Supper did he take on a role that we might recognize as "host." However, from the perspective of the New Testament, hospitality has less to do with welcoming others into a *home* than with welcoming them into a *family*. In other words, Christlike hospitality involves moving someone from the status of "stranger" (a place outside the family) to that of "brother" or "sister" (a place at the heart of the family).[3] In Luke's Gospel, we see Jesus making strangers into family mem-

3. Note that the Greek words *philoxenia* ("hospitality," Rom. 12:13; Heb. 13:2; 1 Peter 4:9) and *philoxenos* ("hospitable," 1 Tim. 3:2; Titus 1:8) may be more literally translated "love for strangers" and "loving toward strangers."

bers on two levels: first, he invites those who are estranged *from God* because of their own sin to return, in faith and repentance, to the Father's embrace; second, he assures those experiencing social, material, and spiritual poverty that they are not relegated to second-class status *within the people of God*. As those who have received such hospitality from Jesus, Christians should be known—as individuals, as families, and as congregations—for their active pursuit of those deemed "strangers" to God and "aliens" to human society.[4]

Like Jesus, you and I should be drawn to those who are deemed too sinful for God's embrace—no matter where their sin falls on the spectrum from notorious immorality to persistent self-righteousness. In our schools, workplaces, and neighborhoods we should pray for a kind of Spirit-given "radar" that would cause us to gravitate toward those who feel unworthy of God's mercy. Our hearts should break to see them outside God's family, and overflow with joy when they accept the Father's forgiveness through trust in Jesus. We should continually be on the lookout for opportunities to display respect toward those outside the Christian faith, drawing "strangers" toward the heart of God's family rather than pushing them further away. To use Luke's language, we should become "friends of sinners."

This is not easy, of course. When we have regular contact with people who happily lead scandalous lives, it is easy to compromise our own commitments, whether by indulging in sin ourselves, or by failing to challenge others to repent. To avoid such compromise requires great wisdom and discernment. In addition, we can anticipate that some Christians will object to our friendship with sinners. I know of a church whose youth ministry began to take seriously their calling to reach out to

4. For a full-length study of Jesus' meal-related hospitality, see Craig L. Blomberg, *Contagious Holiness: Jesus' Meals with Sinners*, New Studies in Biblical Theology 19 (Downers Grove, IL: InterVarsity Press, 2005).

non-Christian teens. As their efforts to welcome "strangers" began to pay off, many in the church—especially parents—grew concerned: "What if these new kids drink or use drugs? What if their language is inappropriate? What do we know about their standards of sexual purity?" Such questions are important, of course, as they recognize that exposing our children to sin can have disastrous consequences. What these questions do not recognize, however, is that it is also disastrous to expose our children—and ourselves—to a form of Christianity that has no concern for Christlike hospitality to those who are estranged from our heavenly Father.

As we saw in chapter 7, Jesus welcomed not only "the lost" but "the least" into the heart of God's purposes. As we grow in likeness to Jesus, we too must demonstrate special concern for those who are treated as inferior or insignificant because they lack status and opportunity in our society. This means that we must learn to discern the insider-outsider boundaries that permeate our daily lives. While such boundaries vary from place to place and from group to group, I mention a few with which we are all familiar:

- *Race/ethnicity*: In the U.S. we know too well the devastating impact of racism and the mistreatment of ethnic minorities. Sadly, this is a worldwide phenomenon, as many Arabs despise blacks in the Sudan, many Scots and English harbor enmity toward each other in Britain, and light-skinned Thais discriminate against those with darker skin.
- *Wealth/education/career*: These three are distinct, but closely related. In Western culture, people with more money and more formal education are "insiders," taken more seriously and given more opportunities. We tend also to judge people based on the prestige of their occu-

pations, and how much success they have achieved in their careers.

- *Age/health*: In general, Western culture is youth oriented, and the elderly are deemed out of touch. However, there are still many circles in which older people hold power and from which younger people are excluded. Sadly, the "worship wars" with which many of us are familiar often put this dividing line on display. Similarly, those who are disabled, chronically ill, or disfigured are often mistreated or overlooked.

Once we have identified such boundaries, we imitate Jesus by refusing to recognize their validity. Practically, this means that we must resist cultural pressures to treat "insiders" as worthy of more dignity and respect than "outsiders," or to see "insiders" as nearer to God's heart, and therefore more significant in his kingdom, than "outsiders." This does not imply that we should dishonor corporate executives, but that we should treat their secretaries, custodial staff, and maintenance crews with the kind of honor we would normally reserve for the executives themselves. We shouldn't despise the pastor of a three-thousand-member suburban church who has published multiple best-selling books—but neither should we consider his ministry more vital to God's kingdom than that of an immigrant who, after three failed attempts to plant churches, oversees a flock of one hundred souls.

One man who challenged such boundaries is J. Robertson McQuilkin, president emeritus of Columbia International University. As president of a school internationally renowned for its role in training missionaries, Dr. McQuilkin's work had a dramatic impact on the work of the gospel around the world. Yet he decided to step down from his position there in order to care full time for his wife, Muriel, whose Alzheimer's disease had worsened. Even when she could no longer recall who he was, Dr. McQuilkin did not see his wife as an "outsider," of less importance than the "insiders" he could train to shape the future of world missions. Instead, he viewed her with great dignity, saying of her in his resignation speech, "She's a delight. It's a great honor to care for such a wonderful person."[5] This is what Christlike passion for the good of others—even those whom the world might consider "the least" and "outsiders"—looks like. As our Savior has extended hospitality to us, may his grace strengthen us to extend it to others!

### *The Second Mark: Accountability*

As our survey in chapter 7 made clear, Jesus often confronts others with the consequences of their actions, whether through calls to repentance, warnings of judgment, or warnings about misplaced priorities. We may conclude, then, that *Christlike passion for the good of others expresses itself in accountability.* While showing hospitality toward the lost and the least, we must also lovingly but honestly challenge others with the realities of sin, judgment, and the radical demands of righteousness.

What might such accountability look like in practice? A few scenarios in which people I know lived out loving, Christlike accountability serve to illustrate key principles:

- *Non-Christians need to hear the call to repent.* Each year the football coach at my high school got to know each student on his team and in his gym classes. Without abusing his position of authority, he took every opportunity to help them hear the gospel—by inviting them to Fellowship

5. A recording of the speech is available at http://www.ciu.edu/robertson-mcquilkin. For more, see Robertson McQuilkin, *A Promise Kept: The Story of an Unforgettable Love* (Wheaton, IL: Tyndale House, 1998).

of Christian Athletes events, inviting them to church, answering their individual questions, or sharing his own testimony of faith in Christ. Some students became Christians through his efforts; others learned through his example what it means to lovingly invite others to turn to Christ.

- *The false confidence of those living in immorality needs to be challenged.* A friend of mine once challenged a colleague, a professing Christian who indulged in wild excesses at weekend parties, to stop living a double life. When it became clear that the colleague refused to change, my friend had no idea what to do—so he arranged for the colleague to meet with a local pastor. Though my friend didn't know what the next step of accountability should look like, he did the loving thing by seeking help from a more mature Christian.

- *The false confidence of the self-righteous needs to be challenged.* While visiting hospitalized church members, Rev. Archie Moore and I chatted with another visitor in the hallway. As she spoke, it became clear that her confidence before God was rooted in her own efforts and accomplishments. At one point she said, "I'm at the church every time the doors are open; that's what it's all about, isn't it?" With a huge smile on his face, and unmistakable warmth, Archie said, "No; it's about Jesus Christ and his righteousness, given to us by the Father—that's what it's all about." Though she was a stranger, Archie loved her enough to confront, gently but clearly, a serious spiritual danger.

- *Maturing believers need to be shown their blind spots.* Another friend once pulled me aside after a meeting at which church leaders were asking me pointed questions

I believed were unfair. He lovingly, but very directly, let me know that as I responded, my body language and my attitude had communicated arrogance, anger, and lack of respect. Through loving confrontation, my friend gave me an opportunity to grow through confession, repentance, and reconciliation.

As the preceding stories demonstrate, loving, Christlike accountability can take many forms. Yet there are barriers that prevent us from pursuing others' good through such confrontation. Shame, failure, or a sense of hypocrisy may make us ask, "Who am I to confront anyone else over matters of sin and obedience? Who am I to hold someone else accountable when I am so imperfect myself?" This question is certainly legitimate, since Jesus warns us not to judge others more harshly than we wish to be judged (Luke 6:37–38), nor to look past our own sins while trying to point out the sins of others (Luke 6:42). But we can carry this legitimate concern to an unhealthy extreme, forgetting that Jesus also said, "If your brother sins, rebuke him" (Luke 17:3). While there is no place for arrogance, condescension, or hypocrisy in our lives, we are called—even with our imperfections—to lovingly challenge others to turn from sin.

Another barrier that may keep us from exercising Christlike accountability is fear of confrontation. Here it helps to remember that as Jesus' followers we must be prepared to be hated, excluded, reviled, and called evil "on account of the Son of Man" (Luke 6:22). Others may accuse us of being unloving, of hating their happiness, even of ruining their lives. But Jesus says, through his teaching and example, that when we hold others accountable we are showing love to them, seeking their joy, even saving their lives. Therefore, while avoiding confrontation may *seem* loving, true concern for the good of others involves extending to them the truth of the gospel—even in its more challenging aspects.

A final reminder is in order. There is the danger that the call to Christlike accountability could be understood as a license for rude, disrespectful, and loveless behavior. But confronting others differs greatly from attacking them, and those whom we challenge with the claims of the gospel should not feel like "targets." Arguing that likeness to Christ is a distinguishing mark of true Christian spirituality, eighteenth-century pastor and theologian Jonathan Edwards addressed this danger:

> [S]ome are much mistaken . . . concerning Christian *zeal*. It is indeed a flame, but a sweet one; or rather it is the heat and fervor of a sweet flame. . . . There is indeed opposition, vigorous opposition, that is an attendant of [zeal]; but it is against *things*, and not *persons*. . . . [Such zeal is] *firstly* and chiefly against . . . the enemies of God and holiness in [the Christian's] own heart . . . and but *secondarily* against the sins of others. And therefore there is nothing in a true Christian zeal contrary to the spirit of meekness, gentleness, and love.[6]

To paraphrase Edwards's point, we might say that even *accountability* must bear the marks of Christlike *hospitality*.

### *The Third Mark: Compassion*

If hospitality and accountability serve as marks that we are growing in our imitation of Christ, they also presuppose a third, overarching truth—namely, that *Christlike passion for the good of others expresses itself in compassion*. We who have experienced the Savior's compassion must share his zeal to relieve those who

6. Jonathan Edwards, "A Treatise Concerning Religious Affections, in Three Parts," 3.8; in *The Works of Jonathan Edwards*, 2 vols. (Edinburgh and Carlisle, PA: Banner of Truth, 1974), 1:306.

are experiencing the miseries of life in a fallen world, whether physical or spiritual. Four foundational commitments can help us to grow in Christlike compassion.

1. *We must join love of sinners with love of sufferers, taking both seriously without minimizing either.* As the parable of the Pharisee and the tax collector (Luke 18:9–14) makes clear, Jesus is concerned that sinners be reconciled to God; as the parable of the good Samaritan (Luke 10:25–37) makes clear, Jesus is equally concerned that mercy be shown to those who suffer. Too often, however, we privilege one form of compassion over the other, failing to recognize that sin creates a range of human needs:

   - As sinners, we experience *guilt, shame, and alienation from God*. Even Christians, who have been reconciled to God through Christ's work, can *feel* that they are estranged from his love.

   - As sinners we also experience what theologians call *corruption*—an enslavement to evil desires that makes it impossible to live God-honoring lives. And even though the Holy Spirit ends this slavery when we turn to Christ, we experience "remaining corruption,"[7] a pervasive, powerful influence that tempts us to live as though sin still had mastery over us.

   - As sufferers, we endure *affliction, sorrow, and pain*. Disease, death, difficulty, and disaster confront us at every turn. Poverty, injustice, crime, mental illness, racism, abuse, war—a heartbreaking and horrifying litany of ills threaten individuals, families, even whole societies.

7. See Westminster Confession of Faith 9.4.

Christlike compassion takes all of these needs seriously, realizing that they are never neatly separable. As a result, we must be prepared to serve others in a wide range of ways, including evangelism (extending compassion by sharing the promises of the gospel), discipleship (extending compassion by encouraging others in their battles against sin's corrupting power), and deeds of mercy (extending compassion by easing the burdens of others). This is not to say that every Christian is equally gifted to minister to every need. But as imitators of Christ, each of our hearts should be sensitive—and ready to respond—to misery in all its forms.

2. *We must be perceptive to the needs of our neighbors.* To exercise Christlike compassion, we must get to know other people—so well, in fact, that they would allow us to help them bear their deepest burdens. On the one hand, this means listening to people around us closely enough to hear the heartbreak behind their words. "Tell me more" may not sound like a particularly loving phrase, but it often opens the door to opportunities to demonstrate profound compassion. On the other, this means becoming aware of our blind spots. For instance, do we assume that our neighbors who have few evident financial needs also have few spiritual or relational problems? Are we quick to help in times of crisis, but slow to recognize ongoing burdens that others bear? As we imitate Christ we will increasingly desire to extend mercy to others, which will in turn make us more attentive to needs that might otherwise be overlooked.

3. *We must actively and wisely resist the power of Satan and demons.* Acts 10:38 says that Jesus "went about doing good and healing all who were oppressed by the devil,"

reminding us that one component of Jesus' compassion was spiritual warfare. For reasons discussed earlier, this does not imply that we should imitate him by performing exorcisms. Yet we should take seriously the existence of Satan and demons, and we should long to see people set free from the miseries they cause. In fact, given biblical descriptions of Satan as a liar (John 8:44) and schemer (2 Cor. 2:11) whose strategies are subtle (2 Cor. 11:3, 14) and whose first deception brought a curse on the entire human race (Gen. 3:1, 15), we should acknowledge that Satan is willing to exploit any instance of human misery. It is wise, then, to pray that all of our efforts at compassion will be bathed in the Spirit's power. And as Jesus prayed for his disciples (Luke 22:32), we must intercede for those whose faith is tested by Satanic assaults. Such prayers remind us that our confidence is not in our own compassion, but in the Savior who has delivered us from all our enemies.

4. *We must cultivate both passion for the good of others and practical expressions of compassion*. It would be ridiculous to believe that we were imitating Christ by doing works of mercy while grumbling, complaining, and hating others in our hearts. It would be equally foolish to think that we could imitate him by constantly theorizing about the importance of compassion without ever actually doing anything for people in need. Christlike commitment to the good of other people will not allow for heart and hands to be divorced. To borrow an image from Jesus, we might say that the healthiest "tree" is one that has a sound root *and* bears "good fruit" (Luke 6:43–45). Thankfully, there is one way to keep the whole tree healthy—namely, by planting it deep in rich, fertile soil. As we are nourished by the truth about our compassionate Savior, both the root of a loving heart and the fruit of loving deeds will grow.

## Conclusion: From Knowing Our Duty to Sharing Our Joy

Having taken a close look at our duty to imitate Christ's passionate commitment to the good of other people, we must ask where we will find the strength to fulfill this duty. For as Luke 10 makes clear, mere knowledge of our duty is not sufficient to prompt obedience; after all, the scribe who approaches Jesus *knows* the biblical requirement to "love . . . your neighbor as yourself" (Luke 10:27), but he does not *want* to love his neighbors—or at least not all of them.[8] What is it, then, that will prompt us to move from knowing our duty to doing it? While chapter 13 will look at this question in more detail, one answer was suggested to me in a recent worship service. Our home church here in St. Louis hosts a "Friendship Class" on Sunday mornings for developmentally disabled adults. Members of the class gave a musical presentation during morning worship, after which several were asked what they like about their class. One young woman with significant mental and physical disabilities answered in speech that was labored, but which made her message crystal clear, "I like Friendship Class because it is a place to learn about Jesus, and to bring your family so they can learn about Jesus." What she was receiving gave her such joy that she wanted others to share it as well. So it is with the good things we receive from our Savior. The love, mercy, and compassion that he extends to us are so good that we want to share them with others—giving ourselves for their good, as Christ has given himself for ours.

8. The command to love neighbor as self comes from Lev. 19:18. As the scribe would have known, the verse makes it clear that "neighbor" includes even those against whom we desire vengeance or bear a grudge; Lev. 19:33–34 goes on to apply the same standard ("you shall love him as yourself") to non-Israelites who live among God's people.

# 9

# Jesus' Willing Denial of Self

IT WAS THE LAST THING we wanted to hear. On December 10, 2011, while all of St. Louis was still euphoric about the Cardinals' improbable World Series win, Albert Pujols officially announced that he would be joining the Los Angeles Angels. No! Tell us anything but that! Tell us our best pitcher, Adam Wainwright, is hurt and out for the entire season (he was). Tell us our future Hall of Fame manager, Tony LaRussa, is retiring (he did). But don't tell us that Pujols is leaving. Tell us anything, but don't tell us that!

American Christians are likely to respond similarly when we read the title of this chapter. Our culture celebrates the "self-made man," the rugged individualist, the pioneer who *asserts* himself. We live in an age where convenience, entertainment, and immediate gratification reign. And our sinful hearts bristle at the thought that there is something about ourselves that needs denying. So tell us anything—but don't tell us we have to deny ourselves! However, willing denial of self is a major feature of Jesus' life, and must be so in our lives if we want to grow in likeness to him. As this chapter will make clear, a closer examination of Jesus' self-denial will deepen our love for him, making us willing and able to imitate this aspect of his character.

## Defining Self-Denial

In Luke 9:23, just after predicting his own death, Jesus issues a call to self-denial: "And he said to all, 'If anyone would come after me, let him deny himself and take up his cross daily and follow me.'" As we noted in chapter 2, the image of cross-bearing presents Jesus' life as the pattern to which his followers should conform. This is true not just for a select few, but for "anyone" who wishes to be his disciple. In this chapter, therefore, we will observe how Jesus models self-denial in Luke's Gospel, so that in chapter 10 we can focus on our calling to imitate this aspect of his example. First, however, we need to know what constitutes self-denial—a concept that is not only profoundly challenging, but easily misunderstood.

As the phrase is popularly employed, the following might be considered examples of self-denial:

- Having one brownie instead of two, even though you're known for your sweet tooth.
- Getting up an hour early each day to make time to care for a sick neighbor.
- Choosing to spend time with family instead of devoting the afternoon to your favorite outdoor activity, even though the weather is perfect.

Notice that each example involves allowing some appetite or desire to go unsatisfied. This reflects the fact that we normally define self-denial as *the opposite of self-indulgence*. However, self-denial actually involves a much more difficult battle. Like a gardener who plucks leaves off a dandelion instead of pulling it up by the roots, it is foolish to think that we have grasped the biblical concept of denying *ourselves* when we are only denying our *desires*.

A deeper understanding of self-denial begins when we notice that Jesus calls us to deny persons—namely, ourselves. What this involves is powerfully illustrated by Peter's denial of Jesus in Luke 22:54–62; we may summarize the text as follows:

- *First denial*: In the courtyard of the high priest's house, a servant girl observes that Peter is one of Jesus' companions. Peter denies it, saying, "Woman, I do not know him."
- *Second denial*: Later, a second bystander observes that Peter is one of Jesus' followers. Peter replies, "Man, I am not."
- *Third denial*: After "about an hour" a third person insists even more forcefully that Peter is a follower of Jesus. Peter responds, "Man, I do not know what you are talking about."
- *Aftermath*: As a rooster crows, Jesus looks at Peter, who remembers Jesus' prediction: "Before the rooster crows today, you will deny me three times." Peter goes out and weeps "bitterly."

Here we must be clear: in this text, Peter is not denying himself, nor is he serving as a positive role model. However, Peter's actions do have something to teach us, since self-denial involves treating *ourselves* the way Peter treats *Jesus*.

In this sobering episode, Peter is essentially saying of Jesus, "I have no allegiance to him. He has no authority over me, no significance for my life, no claims on how I think or live." By analogy, self-denial means saying, "I have no allegiance to myself, to my own purposes and plans. I am not my own authority, and it is not my claims that determine how I think or live." In other words, we deny ourselves when we let someone else—Jesus, in the case of Luke 9:23—define who we are, what we consider most important, and what goals we pursue. In the context of discipleship and cross-bearing, self-denial therefore means saying about ourselves, "The version of me that once took delight in going its own way is unrecognizable to me. That old 'me' has no significance for my life now. The only 'me' I recognize anymore is the one that takes up a cross and follows Jesus."[1]

This kind of allegiance to Christ will of course impact how we exercise our appetites and desires; but such self-control is the fruit of self-denial, not its essence—for as we have seen, self-denial is the opposite not of self-indulgence, but of self-definition. Therefore, to find examples of Jesus' self-denial in Luke's Gospel, we should not ask simply, "Where do we see Jesus controlling his appetites or leaving his desires unfulfilled?" Rather, we must ask, "Where do we see Jesus refusing to conceive of himself apart from God and his purposes? How does allegiance to God, rather than self, shape Jesus' identity, values, and goals?" In the answers to these questions we will find a perfect model of the willing self-denial the Savior requires of us.

## Jesus' Self-Denial and Divine Sonship

An exhaustive study of Jesus' self-denial is impossible, since almost every word of Luke's Gospel shows us how Jesus fulfills God's purposes rather than his own independent priorities. We will therefore focus our attention on three themes:

- Jesus' consistent embrace of his identity as God's Son
- Jesus' faithfulness to a messianic mission that contradicts human expectations
- Jesus' surrender of concern for worldly markers of status, glory, and reputation

1. Compare Gal. 2:20: "I have been crucified with Christ. It is no longer I who live, but Christ who lives in me."

The first of these themes is highlighted in Luke 22:66–71, where Jesus appears before the Jewish ruling council known as the Sanhedrin:

> [A]nd they said, "If you are the Christ, tell us." But he said to them, "If I tell you, you will not believe, and if I ask you, you will not answer. But from now on the Son of Man shall be seated at the right hand of the power of God." So they all said, "Are you the Son of God, then?" And he said to them, "You say that I am." Then they said, "What further testimony do we need? We have heard it ourselves from his own lips."

Jesus' seemingly evasive answers may not immediately strike us as examples of self-denial. But consider the context: Jesus has been arrested, mocked, and beaten (Luke 22:54, 63–65), and is undergoing a hostile interrogation; he now has opportunity to save himself by denying the truth. But in the moment of crisis, knowing that it will lead to his condemnation, Jesus continues to acknowledge that he is Messiah, Son of Man, and Son of God.

Attentive readers of Luke's Gospel will not find this acknowledgment a surprise. From childhood, Jesus has shaped his priorities according to his identity as God's Son; as he says in Luke 2:49, "I must be in my Father's house." At his baptism, he hears his Father affirm, "You are my beloved Son; with you I am well pleased" (Luke 3:22). When Satan later tempts him to exercise his privileges as God's Son in ways that contradict Scripture, Jesus refuses (Luke 4:1–13). At the transfiguration, Jesus once again hears his Father say, "This is my Son, my Chosen One" (Luke 9:35). Thus when the Jerusalem leaders ask, "Are you the Son of God?," something more is at stake than the affirmation of a doctrinal claim. In essence, he is being asked which means more to him—the fact that the Father is "well pleased" with him and has "chosen" him, or the fact that powerful leaders are enraged at him and are rejecting him. By valuing God's testimony more than he fears human judgment, Jesus models self-denial.

Luke's final chapters depict three other events in which Jesus denies himself by embracing his identity as God's Son. First, in the parable of the wicked tenants (Luke 20:9–18), Jesus speaks of a vineyard owner whose "beloved son" is killed; he then cites Psalm 118:22, "The stone that the builders rejected has become the cornerstone." Because he knows that he is the Father's "beloved," Jesus can commit himself to a mission that involves rejection, hostility, and death. Second, Jesus' prayer at Gethsemane makes it clear that he wants God to "remove this cup" (Luke 22:42). But Jesus addresses this request to God as "Father," indicating that his identity, goals, and desires are ultimately shaped by his relationship to God. As a beloved Son should, Jesus wants his Father's will more than his own. Finally, Jesus embraces his relationship to God even when it is turned against him as a taunt during the crucifixion: "He saved others; let him save himself, if he is the Christ of God, his Chosen One!" (Luke 23:35). Even on the cross Jesus does not let his circumstances dictate his identity. If God has said he is "Chosen" (see Luke 9:35), then chosen he remains, though all other evidence may suggest otherwise. Thus Jesus continues to address God as "Father" both when he is crucified (Luke 23:34) and at the moment of his death (Luke 23:46). Others call Jesus to save himself; instead, faithful to his Father's purpose, he denies himself.

## Jesus' Self-Denial and Human Expectations

In addition to a willing embrace of his identity as God's Son, Jesus' self-denial includes letting God's purposes, rather than human expectations, set the agenda for his mission as Messiah. This is especially clear in Luke 9:18–23:

> Now it happened that as he was praying alone, the disciples were with him. And he asked them, "Who do the crowds say that I am?" And they answered, "John the Baptist. But others say, Elijah, and others, that one of the prophets of old has risen." Then he said to them, "But who do you say that I am?" And Peter answered, "The Christ of God."
>
> And he strictly charged and commanded them to tell this to no one, saying, "The Son of Man must suffer many things and be rejected by the elders and chief priests and scribes, and be killed, and on the third day be raised."
>
> And he said to all, "If anyone would come after me, let him deny himself and take up his cross daily and follow me."

As Jesus suffers "many things," endures rejection, and is killed (Luke 9:22), he too is denying himself. By departing from God's intention, Jesus could easily attract crowds hungry for displays of power (Luke 9:19), or recruit more disciples eager to see the messianic king in all his glory (Luke 9:20). Instead, Jesus commits himself to God's purpose, according to which the Christ must first "suffer," and only then "enter into his glory" (Luke 24:26). But this purpose is so contrary to popular expectation that Jesus must warn the apostles not to speak of him as the Messiah (Luke 9:21).[2] Jesus practices self-denial by doing and being what God expects of him, no matter what this may cost in terms of others' misunderstanding or disapproval.

We see this aspect of Jesus' self-denial throughout Luke's Gospel, as Jesus consistently defines his mission according to God's vision, not according to human perspectives that might make him less open to criticism. As his sermon in the Nazareth synagogue shows, being "acceptable in his hometown" (Luke 4:24) matters less to Jesus than being true to God's calling as

2. The potential for misunderstanding explains why Jesus openly and unambiguously identifies himself as the Messiah only after his crucifixion and resurrection (Luke 24:36).

expressed in Scripture. And while you and I might be shaken if crowds appealed for us to stay with them (Luke 4:42), if a prophet like John the Baptist expressed doubts about our ministry (Luke 7:18–23), or if others began to label us gluttons, drunkards, and guilty of keeping immoral company (Luke 7:34), none of these things distracts Jesus from the purpose for which he was sent. Simply put, Jesus is steadfastly committed to a messianic mission that embraces divine, rather than human, priorities.

This point is made clear again in Luke 9:57–62, where Jesus paints a picture of discipleship that makes advancing God's kingdom the highest priority:

> As they were going along the road, someone said to him, "I will follow you wherever you go." And Jesus said to him, "Foxes have holes, and birds of the air have nests, but the Son of Man has nowhere to lay his head." To another he said, "Follow me." But he said, "Lord, let me first go and bury my father." And Jesus said to him, "Leave the dead to bury their own dead. But as for you, go and proclaim the kingdom of God." Yet another said, "I will follow you, Lord, but let me first say farewell to those at my home." Jesus said to him, "No one who puts his hand to the plow and looks back is fit for the kingdom of God."

Though it may discourage some would-be disciples, Jesus says that God's purposes must define us, governing even the way we think about material comforts, personal obligations, and family ties.[3] As the Son of Man who must "suffer many things" (Luke 9:22)—including the trials of a ministry that leaves him with "nowhere to lay his head"—Jesus models this kind of self-denying submission to God.

3. The request to "bury my father" likely amounted to saying, "I'll join you next year, Jesus," since (as the *ESV Study Bible* note indicates) burial involved placing the body in a tomb, then moving the bones to an ossuary a year later.

## Jesus' Self-Denial and Human Greatness

A further aspect of Jesus' self-denial emphasized in Luke's Gospel is his surrender of concern for status and reputation. This is especially highlighted by a series of texts that portray Jesus' closest followers as consistently preoccupied with greatness and glory. To fully appreciate these texts, we must first return to Luke 9:23 to examine the connection between self-denial and cross-bearing.

### *New Priorities: Self-Denial and Cross-bearing*

Like self-denial, cross-bearing is often misunderstood. Today, if we say that a friend "bears her cross" well, we generally mean that she is faithfully enduring some affliction or difficulty that is not of her own choosing—disability, the loss of a loved one, or undeserved criticism, for example. While patience in trials should characterize the Christian life, and we should never make light of affliction, we need to recognize that the image Jesus uses involves something more specific.

First we notice that the cross-bearing Jesus has in mind is active and voluntary. Life does not put this cross on our shoulder; we "take it up" *daily* out of commitment to him. Second, like Jesus' first hearers, we must associate the image of cross-bearing with the realities of crucifixion. A person carrying a cross was a condemned criminal, under a death sentence, carrying his *patibulum* (a beam that would be attached horizontally to a vertical beam to form a cross) to the place of execution. Here, he would be tortured in order to ensure that complete humiliation preceded death. Those sentenced to crucifixion were completely cut off from society, fit only for death (indeed, under God's curse),[4] with no hope of rescue. In this light, Luke

4. For this spiritual aspect of crucifixion, see descriptions of death "on a tree" in Deut. 21:22–23 and Gal. 3:13.

9:23 is Jesus' way of saying, "Denying yourself means living with the priorities of the walking dead. So live like someone whose only hope of rescue is to follow close on my heels—so close, in fact, that the shame, rejection, and humiliation I experience will become a daily feature of your own life." Those who carry a cross define themselves not by greatness and glory, but by their nearness to Jesus.

### *The Apostles' Priority: Concern for Greatness*

Unfortunately, Jesus' followers are frequently consumed with concern for their own greatness. In Luke 9:44–50, while others wonder at Jesus' authority over an evil spirit (Luke 9:43), he says to his disciples, "Let these words sink into your ears: The Son of Man is about to be delivered into the hands of men." The disciples, not only failing to understand but "afraid to ask him about this saying" (Luke 9:45), immediately begin to argue about which of them is greatest. Jesus then uses a child to illustrate God's perspective on greatness, concluding, "For he who is least among you all is the one who is great" (Luke 9:48). The implication is that the disciples fail to understand Jesus' prediction of his death because their identity is wrapped up in concerns about status. Their fear and failure only serve to magnify Jesus' surrender of such concerns as he goes to his death.

We see a similar pattern in Luke 18:31–34, where a third prediction of Jesus' death emphasizes the humiliation he must endure. Jesus says, "See, we are going up to Jerusalem, and everything that is written about the Son of Man . . . will be accomplished. For he will be delivered over to the Gentiles and will be mocked and shamefully treated and spit upon. And after flogging him, they will kill him, and on the third day he will rise." But according to Luke, "They [the apostles] understood none of these things. This saying was hidden from them, and they did not grasp what was said." The word *hidden* (compare "concealed" in Luke 9:45) suggests that there was no way for Jesus' followers to fully understand his words until after his death and resurrection.[5] But the context suggests that the apostles' preoccupation with the rewards of the kingdom (see Luke 18:29) is to blame as well. Jesus draws ever nearer to humiliation and death, but their minds are still fixed on glory.

### *Jesus' Priority: Downward, Difficult Servanthood*

The contrast between the apostles' concern for greatness and Jesus' self-denial is sharpest in Luke 22:24–27. Following the Last Supper, as the Twelve discuss which of them might be Jesus' betrayer (Luke 22:23), an argument breaks out:

> A dispute also arose among them, as to which of them was to be regarded as the greatest. And he said to them, "The kings of the Gentiles exercise lordship over them, and those in authority over them are called benefactors. But not so with you. Rather, let the greatest among you become as the youngest, and the leader as one who serves. For who is greater, one who reclines at table or one who serves? Is it not the one who reclines at table? But I am among you as the one who serves."[6]

Even as Jesus' death approaches, his disciples remain preoccupied with worldly markers of status and perceived greatness. By contrast, Jesus has forsaken such concerns, so that he has less in common with the one who is greater than with "the one who serves."

To fully appreciate Jesus' radical self-denial, and thus the demands of following his example, we must note two features

5. See Luke 24:45, "Then he [Jesus] opened their minds to understand the Scriptures."

6. Similar teaching is found in Matt. 20:25–28 and Mark 10:42–45. However, Luke's text describes a separate event.

of this text. First, we must recognize that the thrust of Luke 22:24–27 is *downward, then outward*. In other words, while we often understand servanthood solely in terms of meeting the needs of other people, Jesus calls for something more challenging. The disciples' dispute focuses on who is greater—who has more desirable societal status, privilege, and recognition. In these terms, when Jesus asks, "Who is the *greater*?" (Luke 22:27), the answer is obvious: the slave owner who reclines to eat is greater than the slave who brings his food and drink. So when Jesus identifies himself with "the one who serves," he is calling his disciples *downward*, to a place of low status, privilege, and recognition—a fitting emphasis, given that the humiliation and shame of the cross are only hours away. This downward thrust does, of course, have a connection with *outward* concern to meet others' needs, for it is impossible to truly love another person if our chief concern is for our own greatness and honor. But that connection involves two steps, not one. To disciples concerned with upward, self-exalting movement, Jesus does not say, "Go outward, as I do," but, "Go down first, humbling yourselves as I do; only then will you be free to go outward, loving others as I do."

Second, we must recognize that the kind of downward-then-outward movement described in Luke 22:24–27 is incredibly difficult. This is evident in the way the text unfolds:

- In Luke 22:24, we observe *the apostles' hearts*, which continue to treasure recognition despite Jesus' repeated rebukes (Luke 9:46–48) and warnings about self-exaltation (Luke 11:43; 14:1–14; 18:9–14; 20:45–47).
- In Luke 22:25, Jesus cites examples from *their culture*, in which political leaders enjoy exalted status (implied in Luke's term for "exercise lordship") and receive honorific titles ("are called benefactors").

- In Luke 22:26–27, Jesus cites examples from *their everyday experience*, in which older people would ordinarily outrank "the youngest," and even routine activities like meals reinforce status distinctions.

Jesus is not asking the apostles to do something that will come naturally. Rather, contrary to what their own hearts and their own culture encourage, he is calling them to give up concern for being recognized as great, instead choosing the lowest place, the place more likely to be despised than admired. This is like asking a retired general to reenlist as a private or a Major League All-Star to sell peanuts in the stands! We know that what Jesus requires is difficult by the weighty argument he must offer as motivation: his own example as "the one who serves."

### *A Pattern of Servanthood*

To more fully understand Jesus' example of self-denial, we must identify the basis of his claim in Luke 22:27. That is, we must ask what features of his life and ministry Jesus appeals to when he says, "I am among you as the one who serves." Several possibilities should be considered. First, many interpreters take Jesus' words to be a reference to all the acts of service he has done throughout his ministry, with a special focus on the way his death will culminate his service to others. As we argued in chapter 7, concern for others is a key theme in Jesus' life, and especially in his sacrifice on our behalf. However, this interpretation neglects the downward thrust that is so prominent in Luke 22:24–27 as a whole. Second, some interpreters take Luke 22:27 as an allusion to the footwashing of John 13, which points ultimately to Jesus' death. A similar interpretation links the meal imagery of Luke 22:27 to Jesus' distribution of bread and wine during the Last Supper. Thus the verse would mean, "Take the lowest place and serve others, as you see me doing in my death, symbolized through the footwashing/the Supper."

The interpretation which seems to me the strongest sees Luke 22:27 as referring to a pattern of servant-like self-humiliation that characterizes Jesus' entire life and ministry. "I am among you as the one who serves" is Jesus' way of saying that his path as Son of God and Messiah has always been marked by suffering, shame, and humiliation rather than by concern for the recognition and privilege that normally accompany greatness. Three factors support this interpretation:

- In Luke 22:26, when Jesus calls the apostles to become "as one who serves," he is calling them to reorient their approach to all of life. It is likely that he has a similar idea in mind when refers to himself in verse 27 using the same phrase (ESV translates "as *the* one who serves," but Luke's Greek is identical).
- Throughout Luke 22:25–27 Jesus refers to relationships (kings-subjects, older-younger, diner/master-servant/slave) that embody ongoing, long-term patterns.
- Luke 12:37 depicts Jesus as the "master" who will reward faithful slaves by having them "recline at table" while he "serve[s]" them (the same verbs as in 22:27). The implication is that the mindset Jesus describes in 22:27 is characteristic not of a particular event or time period, but of who he is *and will continue to be* even after his exaltation.[7]

On this view, Jesus is calling his disciples to imitate him by saying, in effect, "Take the lowest place, the only place from which

7. The point of Luke 12:37 is not that Jesus can be humiliated after his resurrection, but that the exalted Lord remains a king unlike any other—not only humble, but willing to humble himself in order to exalt others.

it is possible to truly love others, as you have seen me doing throughout my ministry, and as you will continue to see me do on the cross—and beyond." Because this pattern is so central to who Jesus is, and because it finds its greatest expression at the cross—which all disciples are called to bear—we may be sure that it is not just Christian leaders but all of Jesus' followers who are called to be like the one who serves.

### *Servanthood and Self-Denial: Three Themes*

The implications of this conclusion for our study are profound. By reminding us that he is one who characteristically takes the lowest place, Jesus invites us not simply to examine his life for particular moments when he denies himself, but to see his entire life and ministry (including his crucifixion) as an embodiment of self-denial. When we do so, we notice three themes in particular:

1. *Jesus never engages in self-exaltation*. While Gentile kings (Luke 22:25), Pharisees and scribes (Luke 14:1–14; 20:46–47), and even his own disciples (Luke 9:46; 22:24) are preoccupied with receiving public recognition of their superiority, Jesus does not play status games. When he displays authority, it is to advance his Father's purposes, not to boost his own ego. Similarly, when Jesus does accept praise and honor from others (as at Luke 5:8; 19:38–40), it is in recognition of a status and calling that he has received from God (Luke 3:22; 4:18; 10:16), not one that he has taken for himself.

2. *Jesus consistently gives up the privileges of "insider" status*. As the Son of God, Jesus is the ultimate insider, entitled to the greatest privileges. Yet when others challenge Jesus to use this status for his own benefit in the wilderness

(Luke 4:1–13) or at the cross (Luke 22:35–39), he refuses. Instead, he identifies with the poor, with sinners, and even with Samaritans (Luke 9:52–56; 10:29–37; 17:11–19) and Gentiles (Luke 4:25–27; 7:9; 13:29; 20:16). In his crucifixion, he becomes the ultimate *outsider*, cursed by God and humiliated by men. While he looks forward to the glory that awaits him (Luke 22:29–30; 23:43; 24:26), Jesus waits for his Father to give it.

3. *Jesus sets aside his own interests for the sake of others.* As the second Adam, Jesus has come not to live for himself, but to reverse the effects of sin and misery for others. In fact, as Jesus remains faithful to this redeeming purpose, he brings more and more suffering upon himself—from the rage of Nazareth (Luke 4:28–29) to the agony of Gethsemane (Luke 22:44) and the darkness of a cursed death (Luke 23:44–46). The "for you" of the Supper (Luke 22:19–20) can become the "with me" of Paradise (Luke 23:43) only because Jesus puts our interests before his own.

The relation of these three themes to self-denial is clear. Jesus' primary allegiance is not to himself—his own status, his own privileges, his own interests. Instead, Jesus' identity, values, and goals are shaped by allegiance to God, and therefore to God's purpose of bringing redemption to needy sinners. For Jesus, being "like the one who serves" meant letting this allegiance to God define every aspect of his life. For us, being "like the one who serves" means letting our allegiance to Jesus so shape us that our lives begin to resemble his.

## Conclusion: *Willing* Self-Denial

As we bring this chapter to a close, you may recall that its topic is *willing* denial of self. This adjective reminds us that the self-denial to which Jesus calls us, and which he models for us, is *glad*, not reluctant, and *voluntary*, not coerced. In Jesus' case, he delights, even in the most difficult of circumstances, to serve his Father alone (Luke 4:8), to do his Father's will (Luke 22:42), and to entrust himself to his Father's hands (Luke 23:46). He has a vision of his Father so glorious, so captivating, that he is willing to pay any cost to remain a faithful Son.

Jesus uses similar logic to motivate us. Thus the call to deny ourselves at Luke 9:23 rests on the assumption that we value Jesus enough to lose our lives for his sake—in fact, that we would rather have the kind of life he gives than the kind of life that would enable us to gain "the whole world" (Luke 9:24–25). The requirements of Luke 22:24–27 rest on the same assumption: on the one hand, the disciples' hearts, the examples they've seen in secular rulers, and the patterns of day-to-day life in their culture encourage them to pursue greatness; on the other, Jesus offers them one reason, and only one, to turn all of this on its head—the fact that he is "like the one who serves." In other words, the radical self-denial to which Jesus calls us is possible only if we conclude that he outweighs everything else put together. With anything less to motivate us, the demands of self-denial would be impossible. But when the one we follow is the Son of God who has taken up his cross for us, we find strength not only to deny ourselves, but to do so *willingly*.

# 10

# Imitating Jesus' Willing Denial of Self

IN A SONG ENTITLED "What Do I Know?," singer-songwriter Sarah Groves seeks to comfort a friend facing death.[1] As the title of the song suggests, she feels inadequate: she is not elderly, she has never faced the fear of death, and she knows nothing of what happens—or is often said to happen—after death. We can certainly identify with her unease; unless we have experienced a similar situation ourselves, what does any of us know about such things? Groves later overcomes her feelings of inadequacy, but only when she recalls the things that Scripture has made clear: 2 Corinthians 5:8 promises that to be "away from the body" is to be "at home with the Lord"; and because we know him, we know that this must be good.

Similar impulses govern the present chapter. A sense of inadequacy might lead us to ask, "What do I know about denying myself—much less about denying myself as Christ did?" But we find confidence in two things that Scripture makes clear: Jesus calls us to take up our cross daily and

1. Sarah Groves, "What Do I Know?," from *Conversations* (Word/Epic, 2001).

follow him on the path of self-denial (Luke 9:23); and he is leading us ultimately to life, even if he first takes us through loss (Luke 9:24–25). To paraphrase Sarah Groves, knowing Jesus convinces us that following him must be good—giving us courage to ask what it would look like for us to imitate his willing denial of self.

In this chapter, we will reflect on three aspects of Christlike self-denial in particular:

- The practice of daily cross-bearing
- The link between self-denial and self-definition
- The lessons we must learn in order to embody servant-like humility

## The Practice of Daily Cross-bearing

In Luke 9:23, Jesus connects self-denial with daily taking up a cross to follow him. With what we learned about this verse in chapter 9 as a backdrop, we may now state more specifically three practical implications of daily cross-bearing, which together form a foundation for the practice of Christlike self-denial.

***1. Cross-bearing requires that we be ready to endure loss and disgrace for Jesus' sake.***

In the ancient world, the cross was an instrument not only of death but of shame. To daily bear a cross behind Jesus, we must therefore be prepared to bear loss (perhaps even loss of life) and to endure shame as a result of our commitment to him. Of course, not every occurrence of loss or shame is an instance of cross-bearing; sometimes these realities come into our lives through our own sin or foolishness, and sometimes through hardships that befall us as human beings rather than as followers of Christ. Jesus calls us to something different, a voluntary choice to share in the loss and disgrace he endures as he goes to the cross on our behalf.

But how would we begin to embody such a choice? Often our thoughts turn to our *circumstances*: Do we need to move to a country where Christians are a persecuted minority whose lives are in danger daily? Do we need to seek a different vocation, one like the young couple I met recently who have borne much loss and disgrace through their ministry to prostitutes? Perhaps our Lord will lead some of us to make such changes in our circumstances; but even these will be the fruit of a deeper change in our *commitments*. In Jesus' day, as in our own, people were committed to avoiding disaster, defeat, and dishonor—the very things represented by the cross. By implication, we are practicing cross-bearing any time we resist the notion that our foremost commitments should be to seeking security, success, and the acclaim of our peers. As imitators of Christ, we are not bound to such commitments, but are free to risk loss, failure, and ridicule.

Practically, this means that dozens of decisions confronting us each day need to be approached with a new kind of logic. As one example, consider the man or woman—whether thirteen, eighty-three, or any age in between—who must decide how to deal with temptations to sexual sin. Given the place unbridled sexuality has in the contemporary worldview, committing oneself for Jesus' sake to the experience of sexual intimacy only within (heterosexual) marriage is the cultural equivalent of wearing a sign that says, "Please mock me, because I am committed to missing out on the very thing that makes life worth living, and I have no interest in being part of the human race." But for disciples of Jesus, things that would normally sound like objections against a given course of action—"This will expose me to what will feel like loss; it is likely to end in what others would see as failure; it may make me a laughingstock, a fool, an object of scorn"—become arguments in its favor, since these are the marks of the cross we are called to bear! Yet as Jesus' command implies, it is only when we are following him that we find the courage to embrace such logic.

### *2. Cross-bearing requires that we renounce all hope in human resources for our salvation.*

The criminal who took up his cross in Jesus' day stood condemned by the Roman Empire, traveling toward death, with no hope of escape. The image of cross-bearing implies that we, like Jesus, must look to God alone for deliverance and blessing. The context of Luke 9:23 confirms that Jesus has such concepts in mind: in Luke 9:22, he speaks of his own death and resurrection; in Luke 9:24–25, he contrasts saving life with losing it, and gaining blessing with forfeiting it; and in Luke 9:26 he contrasts the glory of his return with the shame that will be experienced by those who deny him. Clearly, Jesus expects that God's power will deliver him from death to life, and from the shame of crucifixion to heavenly glory. Similarly, he calls us to trust God alone for what the Bible variously calls "salvation," "eternal life," or "resurrection" life—a life from which sin, sickness, death, and despair are absent, and in which all of God's blessings are perfectly and permanently present.[2]

In April 2012, a Chinese teenager had one of his kidneys removed in an illegal operation, using the money he received to purchase an iPhone® and an iPad®.[3] Being without those gadgets represented to him a curse, and having them represented a state

2. We should note that Scripture applies these terms in different ways, sometimes to describe the final state that God's people will enjoy *in the future*, and sometimes to describe the initial enjoyment of these blessings by God's people *in the present*.

3. "Five charged in Chinese kidney scheme, state media says," CNN.com, http://www.cnn.com/2012/04/06/world/asia/china-kidney (accessed April 10, 2012).

of blessing. This example seems extreme, but it reminds us of our tendency to cling to false hopes, and therefore of the need to wrestle seriously with two questions as we seek to imitate Jesus' dependence on God alone for salvation:

- Negatively, who or what am I trusting to deliver me from death, from shame, and from the divine curse which crucifixion represents?
- Positively, who or what am I trusting to secure for me a perfect and permanent state of blessing?

If we answered honestly, some of us would say, with the young man from China, "possessions and the prestige they bring"; others, "popularity." The more mature might say, "intimate relationships," and the more spiritual, "praiseworthiness before God." In fact, it is easy to view our current life circumstances as a curse, so that the next phase of life becomes our vision of blessedness: "When I get my driver's license . . . When I'm in college . . . When I get married . . . have children . . . retire." Such misplaced hopes indicate that we are still trusting someone or something other than God to save us—as though we were willing to shoulder our crosses only lightly, ready to cast them aside when the next source of salvation comes along. Encouraging us in the discipline of deep and honest repentance is the fact that Jesus' hope in God was not disappointed: after his work on the cross was completed, he was indeed raised!

### *3. Cross-bearing requires that we live with the reoriented priorities of the walking dead.*

The moles in my backyard are a nuisance. And life would be more convenient if our family had a third car. But if I were bearing my own cross to the place of my execution, these matters—and a host of others that feel so important on an average day—would seem utterly insignificant. The weight of the cross on our shoulder is thus intended to provide clarity, enabling us to reorient our understanding of what matters most. Three statements based on Luke 9:23–26 express the reoriented priorities of a disciple who daily takes up a cross to follow Jesus:

- "I will approach all of life as someone who is prepared to die for the cause of Jesus and his kingdom."
- "I treasure Jesus so much that I would rather carry a cross behind him than save my own life."
- "I believe it is safer to follow Jesus to the place of death than to run away."

Such perspectives, which with only minor modifications could be used to describe Jesus' mindset as he went to the cross, remind us once again that self-denial is more than a matter of saying no to certain appetites. To imitate Jesus' willing denial of self, we must treasure something beyond safety and survival as our greatest priority; as Jesus treasured his Father, so we must treasure the Son. When we entrust our safety and security to the one we treasure above all else, then we find freedom to deny ourselves.

## Self-Denial and Self-Definition

As we saw in chapter 9, self-denial is not the opposite of self-indulgence, but of self-definition. In order to practice the kind of self-denial that Jesus did, we must therefore turn away from false standards which so often shape our identity, values, and goals, instead allowing God and his purposes to define the things that are most important to us and about us. In what follows, we present a series of six commitments that help us to pursue this twin purpose practically. The commitments themselves employ singular pronouns (I, my) to remind us that self-denial must be practiced by each individual follower of Jesus; however, the discussion of each commitment mixes these with plural pronouns (we, our), reminding us that we will need the support of Christian brothers and sisters if we are to seriously pursue Christlike denial of self.

***Commitment 1: I will not define myself according to my group status.***

Many identity markers are ours at birth, such as gender, race, ethnicity, socioeconomic status, linguistic group, or family background. While such markers are not without value—many of them expressing the wonderful diversity of God's image-bearers—they do not mark what is most important about a Christian. Our boast is not that we are of African or European descent, that we are Americans or Mexicans, that we are male or female, or that we come from a long line of Presbyterians, charismatics, or atheists. Our boast is that we belong to Jesus, through whom we are being renewed in the image of God (Col. 3:10–11). Similarly, inherited status cannot define us negatively, whether by relegating us to second-class citizenship in God's kingdom or dooming us to repeat the sins of our ancestors. According to Jesus, all who follow him are royalty, heirs of their Father's kingdom (Luke 6:20–23).

Other identity markers come from groups with which we have chosen to associate: we go to this college, choose that career path, move to that neighborhood; become Republicans, Democrats, or Independents; get involved with a particular civic club, social cause, or recreational activity. We even choose what denomination, what congregation, or what ministry team within a congregation to be a part of. Again, none of these is our core identity. If we are clinging tightly to Christ, we will hold such affiliations loosely—not because they are unimportant, but because they are not most important.

***Commitment 2: I will not define myself according to my accomplishments.***

If my identity is shaped around God, then the accomplishments that will matter most to me are those of his Son, for it is Christ's work that determines where I stand in relation to God and to other people. But our hearts and our culture will pressure us to define ourselves according to our own accomplishments, not our Savior's. On this approach, our identity lies in the answers to three questions: What have I earned? What have I produced? What have I achieved? By implication, those who have earned/produced/achieved more are superior to their neighbors and more acceptable to God.

Jesus warns of these dangers in parables: pride in our religious accomplishments can cause us to look down on others (Luke 18:9–14, the Pharisee and the tax collector); yet we could not merit God's favor even if we did everything that he requires of us (Luke 17:7–10, unworthy servants). Self-denial means confiding in God's mercies, not defining ourselves by our successes—or lack thereof. And as Jesus makes clear, such confidence actually leads to greater accomplishment, whether in the form of more lavish love for God/Jesus (Luke 7:41–50), willingness to risk more in his service (Luke 19:11–27), or greater generosity (Luke 21:1–4).

***Commitment 3: I will not define myself according to reputation or appearance.***

Even in the Upper Room, Jesus' disciples defined themselves according to reputation, arguing about "which of them was to be regarded as greatest" (Luke 22:24). To see that we do the same thing, we need only recall how often we ask ourselves, "Are other people impressed with me?" Sometimes we seek to impress a group of people (friends, neighbors, classmates, teammates) and sometimes an individual (a spouse, a parent, a rival at work, a peer whose respect we crave). Either way, much of our time and energy is spent trying to gain the attention and approval of others. As with the disciples in the Upper Room, the antidote is for us to fix our attention on Jesus: "But I am among you as the one who serves" (Luke 22:27).

Closely related to hunger for reputation is the temptation to seek others' approval through physical appearance. Western culture's current infatuation with youth means that any signs of aging must be masked or mended. Beauty products and fitness programs abound, often implying that we are somehow inadequate unless we look like *this*—ignoring the fact that no one, not even the model whose digitally enhanced image we see, looks like that. Self-denial means that what matters most to us is not our appearance, but the perspective of our God, who looks not "on the outward appearance, but . . . on the heart" (1 Sam. 16:7).

***Commitment 4: I will not define myself according to what I possess, enjoy, lose, or lack.***

Another false source of identity is lifestyle. All of us know that what we own, what vacations we can afford, how much leisure time we have and how we spend it, are not the most important things about us. Yet we often act otherwise, engaging in conspicuous consumption, envying others' blessings, and failing to show gratitude for the good gifts God has given us. By God's mercy, real contentment is possible—but only when our identity is found in Christ. Or, to use the language of Luke's Gospel, "where your treasure is, there will your heart be also" (Luke 12:34).

Sadly, when we define ourselves by what we possess, enjoy, lose, or lack, we become slaves to our desires. If our identity hinges on such matters, then fear will drive us to indulge every appetite: "What if I never get to experience the satisfaction of fully venting my anger, my lust, my greed? What if everybody else is living the good life, and I'm missing out?" Behind such fears is the assumption that the most important thing about us is what we do or don't enjoy, what we do or don't experience. Jesus says this is a lie. The most important thing about us is whether we follow him, losing our lives for his sake, and ultimately receiving more from him than we could ever gain for ourselves.[4]

***Commitment 5: I will value God's testimony about me more than I fear anyone's judgment against me.***

Before the Sanhedrin, with his own life at stake, Jesus refuses to deny what his Father has affirmed—namely, that he is the Son of God (Luke 22:70–71). Similarly, self-denial requires that we treasure what our Father says is true of us, even when others—whether individuals, groups, cultural systems, or Satan himself—speak judgment against us. Sometimes these voices of judgment condemn us: "You have disregarded too many of God's commandments for too long; you can never be forgiven!" At other times they threaten us with ostracism, ridicule, or worse: "If you take this Jesus too seriously, you can have nothing to do with us. If you choose him, we will take everything away from you—maybe even your life!" More subtly, these voices may seek to paralyze us through fear and anxiety: "Fool! What good will this religion be when bills aren't paid, there is no money in the bank, and real-world responsibilities go unmet?"

But God's testimony about us, spoken through his Son, overpowers such voices. Once we were rebels, cut off from God and his blessings, but now we are beloved children in whom our Father delights (Luke 15:11–32). Once we were lost sheep, wandering from God's ways, but now the strong Shepherd has

4. This confirms what we suggested in chapter 9: while self-denial cannot be reduced to controlling one's appetites, it does bear the fruit of self-control.

laid us on his shoulders and brought us home, rejoicing (Luke 15:3–5). Enemies can take from us what they will, but our Father values us so much that not even a hair of our heads will perish (Luke 12:6–7; 21:18). The world may scorn us, but our Father has pronounced us "blessed" (Luke 6:22). When we define ourselves as God does, we can answer every judgment against us with the promises he has spoken.

***Commitment 6: I will pursue God's vision for me rather than conforming to human expectations of me.***

As you may notice, this single statement is an umbrella under which the five previous commitments fit. Still, it is worth giving special attention to a broader tension between God's vision for us and human expectations. In Jesus' life, this tension often centers on the question of what it means to be Messiah; for you and me, however, it tends to center on the question of what it means to be human. God's answer is clear in Genesis 1–2: being human means bearing God's image faithfully, and therefore being in relationships of life and love with him, with our fellow human beings, and with the created world. Since the first sin of Genesis 3, God's vision for us also includes a new stage that will restore what human rebellion has destroyed and distorted, a stage in which "all flesh shall see the salvation of God" (Luke 3:6). Simply put, God's vision for you and for me is that we would be part of his mission to redeem the world.

Note that this vision is simultaneously ambitious and humble. On the one hand, it is global in scope and cosmic in consequence: we are part of a worldwide movement to liberate fallen image-bearers from God's condemnation, from the enslaving power of sin and Satan, and from the miseries that afflict all of creation. On the other, the success of this mission depends on God's strength, and not our own (Luke 17:5–6; 18:26–27), and our place in it is due to his mercy, not our qualifications (Luke 15:1–32; 17:7–10; 18:9–14). By contrast, human expectations typically encourage us to be ambitious or humble, but not both. Some people expect us to be "movers and shakers" who magnify human power or "visionaries" who magnify human potential—but they encourage us to change the world by remaining independent of God and his purposes. Others expect us to think on a more limited, individual scale—as though our purpose in living were to build a private kingdom in which personal priorities are met and material comforts are enjoyed. To such expectations, Christlike self-denial says, "Rubbish"—for none but the God who made us and redeemed us can set the vision that governs our lives.

## Learning Servant-Like Humility

As we noted in chapter 9, and as our discussion of resisting human expectations implies, self-denial involves turning away from preoccupation with our own status, privileges, and interests. We therefore close this chapter with three lessons we must learn in order to imitate the downward-then-outward pattern of servant-like humility that we observe in Jesus.

### *Lesson 1: Learning to Put Ourselves Last*

Appealing to his own example, Jesus calls the apostles to become "as the youngest" and "as one who serves" (Luke 22:24–27). Rather than clamoring to be greatest or first, we must take the place that is lowest and last. Practically, this means that we must resist three patterns associated with self-exaltation:

- *A preoccupation with rank or reputation based on comparison to other people*: The self-exalting Pharisee of Luke 18:11 prays, "God, I thank you that I am not like other men"; similarly, Jesus' apostles are concerned with which of them is greatest in comparison with the others (Luke 9:46–48; 22:24–27). We can be sure that we are moving away from Christlike humility when we begin to measure ourselves against others. We are on safer ground when we ask, "Where do I stand in relation to God and his Son?"

- *A preoccupation with markers of superior status, power, or position*: In Jesus' world, such markers included long robes, formal public greetings, seats of honor in public settings, titles such as "benefactor," and even age (see Luke 11:43; 14:7–11; 20:46; 22:24–27). In our day, they include general categories such as wealth, career, education, and physical appearance, and more specific markers like what we wear, what we drive, and what gadgets we own. If we find ourselves keeping track of who has or doesn't have the "right" markers—or of who has noticed the markers we have—we have embraced the mindset of self-exaltation rather than that of servanthood.

- *A craving for public recognition*: While it is not wrong to desire encouragement, affirmation, and even praise, we must receive these as gifts rather than demand them as our due. The parable in Luke 14:7–11 demonstrates the point: choosing a place of honor for ourselves is wrong, but being moved to a higher seat by the host (representing God) is not. When we begin to feel that we deserve more recognition than we are receiving, we are departing from the lowliness displayed by Christ, who did "enter into his glory" (Luke 24:26), but only when his Father's purposes and timing were fulfilled.

Putting ourselves last means demonstrating by our lives that our first allegiance is not to rank, superiority, or recognition, but to the Savior who put himself in the lowest place for us. Thus, when self-exalting attitudes threaten to weigh down our hearts, we must repentantly pray for strength (see Luke 21:34–36) to deny ourselves instead.

### *Lesson 2: Learning to Put Others First*

Luke's crucifixion account makes it clear that Jesus refuses to save himself precisely because he has come to save others (Luke 23:35–39). While we can never duplicate the wonder of Jesus' self-sacrificial love, we can reflect his servant-like love of neighbor by putting others first in two ways:

- *By seeing people as God sees them*: When we put ourselves first, we tend to see other people in one of three categories: as obstacles, preventing us from reaching our own goals or meeting our own needs; as competitors, threatening to take away the recognition or resources we desire for ourselves; or as tools, serving the ends we choose. But we put others first when we see them as God's image-bearers, to be treated in a way that pleases him; as fellow sinners who, like "all flesh," need to "see the salvation of God" (Luke 3:6); and as fellow sufferers, neighbors in need of mercy (Luke 10:25–37).
- *By giving away honor and privilege*: In Luke 14:7–14, Jesus rebukes the guests at a banquet for seeking honor for themselves, and he rebukes the host for securing his own privileged status by excluding the poor and disabled. By contrast, Christlike humility entails sharing whatever honor we have with those who have none, and yielding the privileges of "insider" status by welcoming "outsiders." As his mercy transforms us, we become increasingly aware of those around us who are overlooked, excluded, mistreated, or in need—and of

opportunities we have to affirm, encourage, welcome, and serve them.

An Indian pastor once challenged a friend of mine with a vivid metaphor: "You Americans are all alike," he said. "You always want to be at the front of the line." Jesus' servant-like humility calls us to do just the opposite—to go to the back of the line, and to put the people we find there first, sharing with them the kind of honor, privilege, and selfless love Jesus has lavished on us.

### *Lesson 3: Learning to Treasure God Most*

To understand this third lesson in Christlike humility, we may consider the analogy of running a marathon: to put one foot in front of the other for 26.2 miles is not a natural task, since most experts agree that the human body is designed to run only about 20 miles. Yet every year, hundreds of thousands of runners find some goal—fitness, a sense of accomplishment, companionship with other runners—so compelling that they push themselves beyond what seems possible. Likewise, since the sinful human heart desires to put *self* first, maintaining the two-step rhythm of putting ourselves last and others first feels unnatural. To sustain us when this calling seems impossibly difficult, we need a compelling motive. Self can become last, and others first, only when God is treasured most.

To grow as imitators of Christ, we must particularly learn to:

- *Treasure God's wisdom*: According to human wisdom, it is difficult to believe that what is best for others is also what is best for me. But if God says it is best for me to delay my trip to Jericho in order to extend mercy to someone in need (Luke 10:25–37), I have to believe him. And if he promises to exalt me when I humble myself, I must trust the wisdom of his timing—even if it means waiting until "the resurrection of the just" (Luke 14:7–14). If his wisdom has provided for our salvation through his Son, then it is not only to be trusted, but treasured.

- *Treasure God's wealth*: Behind Jesus' teaching about self-exaltation, and behind his example of servant-like humility are two presuppositions. First, whatever honor or status we could get for ourselves is worthless, while that which God gives is infinitely and eternally valuable. Second, God's supplies of honor and love are limitless, so that we are free to give away as much as he calls us to, without fearing that he will leave us destitute. Knowing that our Father possesses these true riches in infinite supply, we can gladly give up meaningless markers of greatness, and freely bestow real love on those who need it most. To use Jesus' imagery, if we know that we will one day "recline at table in the kingdom of God" (Luke 13:29; see also 12:37; 22:29–30), then we are free now to join Jesus, who gives up his place at table to take the place of the servant (Luke 22:27).

We see these patterns of humility and servanthood—putting self last, putting others first, and treasuring God most—throughout Jesus' life. Yet they are most powerfully expressed at the cross, where he simultaneously takes the place of greatest shame, fulfills his purpose to save others rather than himself, and demonstrates the full extent of his love for the Father. If we would deny ourselves, bear our crosses daily, and follow Jesus, we too must become like "the one who serves."

## Conclusion: Running the Race

By now it should be clear that our earlier marathon analogy was woefully inadequate. As we have seen in this chapter, the race we run is more like a spiritual triathlon, combining three activities, any one of which is enough to push us beyond our limits: daily cross-bearing; denying ourselves by defining ourselves according to divine, rather than human, standards; and learning the kind of servant-like humility we see in Jesus. And while even the longest endurance races last only a few hours, we must run this course for the rest of our lives. Thankfully, we are not running this race alone, but in the footsteps of our Savior. Though smoother paths tempt us, and weariness discourages us, we continue to run—knowing that every step we take on this path of self-denial brings us nearer to Jesus, who took up his cross, sacrificed himself, and humbly served us.

# 11

# Jesus' Patient Endurance of Hardship

"IT'S THE COMBINATION that kills you." My friend Charlie said those words as he, I, and our daughters faced a steep climb on the Ozark Trail in southeastern Missouri. It was early June, with temperatures in the nineties, and the sun was roasting us as we climbed away from trees—and shade. An experienced backpacker, Charlie was observing that it is challenging to carry a heavy pack uphill, and challenging to carry a heavy pack in the hot sun. But when you put the two together, "challenging" is no longer an adequate description. Words like *wearying*, *withering*, even *demoralizing* seem more appropriate. On its own, either challenge could be managed. But the combination—well, as Charlie said, it kills you.

So it is when we come to the topic of this chapter. To endure hardship is in itself a challenge. And to wait patiently for some hoped-for outcome is equally challenging. But to patiently endure hardship is the kind of wearying task that, spiritually speaking, can drain the life out of us. Yet in the example of Jesus, we find hope that such patient endurance really is possible. Like us, Jesus experienced difficult circumstances that resulted in distress, weakness, weariness, and suffering. Unlike us, he always endured such hardships with calmness and gentleness rather than with anger, complaint, bitterness, or irritation.

To demonstrate more concretely how Jesus responds to hardship with patient endurance rather than with the priorities typical of sinful human beings, this chapter will employ a series of four contrasts:

- Contentment versus comfort
- Courage versus cowardice
- Gentleness versus anger
- Compassion versus retaliation

As we will discover, looking to Jesus' example does not take away the difficulty of patiently enduring hardship. But it does remind us that when the path of life takes an uphill turn into withering heat, we are not alone. The hill has already been climbed by our Savior, whose life—and death—call us to follow him on a path of patient endurance.

## Contentment versus Comfort

A glance at ads on television, in magazines, and on billboards reveals one of the assumptions of contemporary American culture—namely, that people should strive for as much comfort and pleasure as possible. This assumption was shared by kings and authority figures in Jesus' day as well. By contrast, Luke's Gospel portrays Jesus as someone who is content with what his Father has provided. Rather than pursuing comfort and pleasure, Jesus finds his satisfaction in doing God's will, even in the face of the greatest hardships ever endured.

### *Jesus' Call to Contentment*

We expect Jesus to model contentment with God's provision, rather than a pursuit of his own comfort, because his teaching emphasizes this contrast. He warns us that our lives will never bear fruit if we are "choked by the cares and riches and pleasures of life" (Luke 8:14), and that our hearts can be "weighed down" not only by drunken pursuit of pleasure but by concern for daily needs (Luke 21:34). Rather than worrying about material provision such as food and clothing, we are to seek God's kingdom, trusting him to supply what we need (Luke 12:22–31). Likewise, contentment with God's provision means that we no longer seek to prove that we outrank others; instead, we humble ourselves, trusting God to exalt us as he pleases (Luke 9:46–48; 11:43; 14:7–14; 18:14; 20:45–47; 22:24–27). To be a disciple of Jesus, then, is to be content with poverty, hunger, weeping, and rejection in the present, because we trust that our Father will one day bless us beyond measure (Luke 6:20–26; see also 18:28–30).

### *Jesus' Key to Contentment*

To help us appreciate Jesus' own contentment in the midst of hardship, we may look first to Luke 24:13–27, where we find two contrasting interpretations of his suffering. According to the unnamed disciples Jesus encounters on the road to Emmaus, Jesus' suffering proves that he was not the Messiah. Not yet recognizing the identity of the risen Lord, these disciples summarize recent events in Jerusalem for him: "[O]ur chief priests and rulers delivered him [Jesus] up to be condemned to death, and crucified him. But we had hoped that he was the one to redeem Israel" (Luke 24:19–21). Yet when Jesus responds, he speaks of suffering as an integral part of his calling as Messiah: "And he said to them, 'O foolish ones, and slow of heart to believe all that the prophets have spoken! Was it not necessary that the Christ should suffer these things and enter into his glory?'" (Luke 24:25–26).

As these words remind us, Jesus speaks of his coming suffering many times before his death. Immediately after being identified by Peter as "the Christ of God" (Luke 9:20), Jesus says,

"The Son of Man must suffer many things and be rejected by the elders and chief priests and scribes, and be killed, and on the third day be raised" (Luke 9:22). Similar predictions occur just after Jesus' transfiguration (Luke 9:44), as he discusses his glorious return (Luke 17:25), and just before the triumphal entry into Jerusalem (Luke 18:31–33). As the Messiah, Jesus possesses royal authority, and is the rightful heir of a glory that transcends this earth. But in the minds of his disciples, accustomed to kings who live in luxury and raise armies to ensure their own survival, this implies that Jesus is immune to, or at least should make every effort to avoid, suffering and death. The overall portrayal of Jesus is therefore shocking: here is a king who rejoices to fulfill God's saving purpose, even if this means he must endure agonizing suffering before he tastes the glory promised by his Father. For Jesus, the key to contentment is dedication to his Father's purpose, which involves both suffering and glory.

### *Jesus' Contentment in Crisis*

While we have already observed other aspects of Jesus' character revealed in his temptation, his prayer at Gethsemane, and his crucifixion, these key events also shed further light on Jesus' contentment with his calling. Note, for instance, the assumption behind the first and third temptations Jesus confronts in the wilderness (Luke 4:1–13). When Satan says, "If you are the Son of God, command this stone to become bread" (Luke 4:3), he assumes that Jesus' status as Son of God should lead him to minimize, rather than endure, hardship and deprivation. Similarly, twisting the promise of Psalm 91, Satan assumes that if Jesus is the Son of God, he can throw himself from "the pinnacle of the temple" without fear of injury (Luke 4:9–11). Jesus knows, however, that the security promised in Psalm 91 is found not by doing Satan's bidding, but by doing his Father's will, which leads him *first through suffering* and then to glory. When Jesus rejects

Satan's temptations, we see that he is content to pursue his calling as Redeemer, though it will ultimately cost him his life.

In Gethsemane, Jesus again models contentment and endurance, though his initial request—"Father, if you are willing, remove this cup from me" (Luke 22:42)—raises important questions. Is Jesus' contentment with pursuing God's purpose wavering? Has his supply of patient endurance reached its limits? The answer is complex. On the one hand, Jesus is honestly grappling with the weight of the agony that is before him. Rather than pretending that it is pleasant, Jesus directly acknowledges the depth of suffering that will be required of him—and his honest preference to avoid it if possible. On the other hand, Jesus expresses his honest grappling in a submissive way: "Nevertheless, not my will, but yours, be done" (Luke 22:42). Whatever he might prefer, Jesus' deepest desire is to do his Father's will. Ultimately, then, Jesus' prayer at Gethsemane represents not a weakening of his commitment to endure hardship, but a final preparation for the anguish that lies ahead.

Jesus' resolve to endure hardship reaches its climax in his crucifixion, where we once again encounter the assumption that royal status should make Jesus immune to suffering. Just as Satan tempted Jesus three times in the wilderness, so three times Jesus is challenged to spare himself the humiliation and torture of the cross:

- *Luke 23:35*: "[T]he rulers scoffed at him, saying, 'He saved others; let him save himself, if he is the Christ of God, his Chosen One!'"
- *Luke 23:36–37*: "The soldiers also mocked him . . . saying, 'If you are the King of the Jews, save yourself!'"
- *Luke 23:39*: "One of the criminals who were hanged railed at him, saying, 'Are you not the Christ? Save yourself and us!'"

These challenges assume that no king, whether Roman or Jewish, would endure such suffering and humiliation if it was truly in his power to stop it. But Jesus resists such logic and remains confident that God will receive him into "Paradise" (Luke 23:43). By his endurance of the cross, Jesus shouts, "I look forward to being in Paradise with my Father, when the suffering and sorrow of this cross will be ended. But I would rather stay here on his terms than come down on yours!" Jesus does not despise comfort; but trust in his Father's promises, and commitment to his Father's purposes, allows him to endure even the worst suffering imaginable.

## Courage versus Cowardice

To go to a cross knowing that you will face the wrath of God and the mockery of men requires not only contentment, but great courage. When Jesus displays such courage, he is modeling what he requires of his followers in Luke 12:4–12. As hostility from the scribes and Pharisees increases, Jesus urges his disciples not to "fear those who kill the body" (Luke 12:4), not to yield to pressure to deny him before men (Luke 12:9), and not to be anxious about what to say when brought before hostile authorities (Luke 12:11). The implication is that opposition and persecution tempt us to cowardice. In fact, the temptation is so profound that only divine resources—our worth before God (Luke 12:7), Jesus' promise to acknowledge us (Luke 12:8), and the Holy Spirit's presence (Luke 12:12)—can sustain our courage. Here, then, we examine Jesus' courage in the face of criticism, rejection, and persecution.

### *Jesus' Courageous Response to Early Opposition*

The first indication we have of Jesus' courage despite opposition comes in his synagogue sermon at Nazareth (Luke 4:16–30). Despite knowing that he is not "acceptable in his hometown"

(Luke 4:24), Jesus concludes his sermon on a note that provokes the wrath of his hearers, reminding them that God's purpose includes extending mercy to Gentiles—even to those like "Naaman the Syrian" (Luke 4:27; see 2 Kings 5:1–14). Given that the Syrian king Antiochus IV had brutally persecuted Jews only two hundred years earlier (even erecting an altar to Zeus in the temple), and that Israel had been occupied by Gentile powers ever since, Jesus' insistence that God's mercy extends to hated Gentiles demonstrates great courage. And while the crowd's response—driving Jesus toward a cliff so that they might kill him (Luke 4:29)—might convince many preachers to remain quiet, the next we hear of Jesus he is once more teaching in a synagogue (Luke 4:31).

As Luke's Gospel unfolds, Jesus faces continued opposition from Pharisees and scribes, who accuse him of blasphemy (Luke 5:21), of violating the Sabbath (Luke 6:2, 7), and of inappropriate association with "tax collectors and sinners" (Luke 5:27–30; 7:34, 39). Rather than compromise his commitment to God's merciful purposes, Jesus continues to extend forgiveness, and even fellowship, to those deemed unworthy. As at Nazareth, such courage eventually prompts open hostility, as the Pharisees and scribes are "filled with fury" and begin to consider "what they might do to Jesus" (Luke 6:11).

### *Jesus' Courage on the Path to Jerusalem*

Jesus' courage is especially evident at Luke 9:51: "When the days drew near for him to be taken up, he set his face to go to Jerusalem." Before Jesus can be "taken up" (a reference to his ascension into heaven; see Acts 1:2, 11, 22), he must first face death in Jerusalem, where he will be rejected by "the elders and chief priests and scribes" (Luke 9:22). Fully aware of the consequences, Jesus firmly resolves—Luke's phrase "set his face" is equivalent to the English idiom *steeled his jaw*—to follow the path God has appointed. Jesus' courage is highlighted by the apostles' fear; when Jesus predicts that he will be "delivered into the hands of men," they are "afraid to ask him about this saying" (Luke 9:44–45).

How firmly is Jesus' face "set"? We find out when Jesus is warned by a group of Pharisees that Herod Antipas, who is already responsible for the death of John the Baptist (Luke 9:9), is seeking to kill him (Luke 13:31–34). Jesus agrees that he must leave Herod's territory, though not to escape death: "Nevertheless, I must go on my way . . . for it cannot be that a prophet should perish away from Jerusalem," the city that "kills the prophets and stones those who are sent to it!" (Luke 13:33–34). To Jesus, a king who makes death threats is no more intimidating than a fox (Luke 13:32). Some people may put their hands to the plow and look back (Luke 9:62), but Jesus is not one of them.

### *Jesus' Courage to the End*

The ultimate depiction of Jesus' courage occurs once he reaches Jerusalem. There, Jesus continues to directly confront those who are plotting his destruction (Luke 19:45–20:26), though they are afraid to take a public stand against him (see Luke 20:19–20; 22:1). Knowing that he will be betrayed by Judas, denied by Peter, and "numbered with the transgressors" despite his innocence (Luke 22:37, citing Isa. 53:12), Jesus does not flee, panic, or despair. He prays, submitting his desires to his Father's purpose, and he answers his accusers' questions in ways that increase, rather than diminish, his danger (Luke 22:66–23:3). Finally, Jesus three times refuses the temptation to save himself on the cross—a sharp contrast to the cowardice of Peter, who three times protects himself by denying Jesus. Jesus' courage is displayed not in his willingness to take up swords against his enemies (Luke 22:38, 49–50), but in his willingness to endure hostility at their hands, so that God's mercy to sinners might be multiplied.

## Gentleness versus Anger

Our natural impulse when we are rejected and insulted is anger and indignation. Yet in Luke 6:22–23, Jesus speaks a hard word to his disciples: "Blessed are you when people hate you and when they exclude you and revile you and spurn your name as evil, on account of the Son of Man! Rejoice in that day, and leap for joy, for behold, your reward is great in heaven." Similarly, our natural impulse when sinned against is to grow bitter, to nurse resentment, and to continue extracting payment from those who have offended us. Again, Jesus speaks a hard word in Luke 17:3–4: "Pay attention to yourselves! If your brother sins, rebuke him, and if he repents, forgive him, and if he sins against you seven times in the day, and turns to you seven times, saying, 'I repent,' you must forgive him." Jesus teaches us to respond with gentleness, joy, and forgiveness when we are mistreated or offended. Here we examine how Jesus models such a response to those who hate, reject, and sin against him.

### *Jesus' Response to Betrayal and Denial*

We learn much about Jesus' character from the way he responds when sinned against by two of his closest followers. In the case of Judas, whose betrayal leads to Jesus' arrest, Jesus predicts the betrayal itself, then comments, "For the Son of Man goes as it has been determined, but woe to that man by whom he is betrayed!" (Luke 22:22). On the one hand, we see here Jesus' honest assessment of sin, as the betrayal will bring "woe" (a word that implies divine judgment) upon Judas. On the other, we see his gentleness—for what kind of rabbi allows a betrayer to share his table at Passover? Or what kind of king (see the kingship language in Luke 22:25, 29–30) invites an enemy to a feast? Similarly, Jesus' response to Judas at the moment of betrayal displays remarkable self-control. Rather than a lengthy, bitter tirade, Jesus simply asks, "Judas, is it with a kiss that you are betraying the Son of Man?" (Luke 22:48, translation my own). Again Jesus acknowledges the painful reality of Judas's sin, but responds with gentleness even though a more hostile reaction would seem justified.

Jesus responds in a similar way to Peter's sin against him. In Luke 22:34, Jesus predicts that Peter will deny him three times before the night is through. Jesus' words are hard for Peter to hear (see Luke 22:33), but they are not overly harsh, vindictive, or designed to humiliate. In fact, knowing full well that Peter will deny him, Jesus has already prayed for Peter, and is willing for Peter's role as a leader to continue: "Simon, Simon . . . I have prayed for you that your faith may not fail. And when you have turned again, strengthen your brothers" (Luke 22:31–32). As he requires of us, Jesus is willing to forgive one who "turns" after sinning multiple times in the same day (Luke 17:3–4).

This shapes the way we understand Luke 22:61, where, after recounting Peter's threefold denial, Luke writes, "And the Lord turned and looked at Peter. And Peter remembered the saying of the Lord." Jesus' gentleness and forgiving spirit do not cause him to ignore sin. In this case, too far across the courtyard of the high priest's house to speak to Peter, Jesus confronts Peter with a glance. But instead of crushing or condemning, this glance initiates Peter's restoration by prompting him to repentance (see Luke 22:62). The one who knows Peter's sin is also ready to forgive.

### *Jesus' Patience with Persistent Misunderstanding*

Jesus' dealings with Peter call to mind many other occasions when the apostles have grieved Jesus, not through overt rejection but through persistent failure to grasp the truth about him. The Twelve fail to trust Jesus during the storm on the Sea of Galilee (Luke 8:25, "Where is your faith?"), and when they are afraid to ask him what he means by predicting his death (Luke 9:44–45; see also 18:31–34), they go on instead to argue about which of them is greatest (Luke 9:46). Despite Jesus' use of a child to teach them that he does not calculate greatness as they do (Luke 9:47–48), the apostles hinder parents who are bringing their children to Jesus (Luke 18:15), and even in the Upper Room they continue to wrangle over who is "regarded as the greatest" (Luke 22:24). Yet Jesus never gives up on his disciples. He does not dismiss them as hopeless, berate their spiritual thickheadedness, or condemn them with disparaging remarks. In fact, after correcting their concern for greatness at the Last Supper, Jesus commends his disciples as "those who have stayed with me in my trials," and he promises them leading roles in his coming kingdom (Luke 22:28–29).

Jesus' strongest expression of frustration with his disciples occurs in Luke 9:41. Here, after learning of the disciples' inability to cast out an evil spirit from a child, Jesus cries out, "O faithless and twisted generation, how long am I to be with you and bear with you?" The word *bear* suggests that it requires patience and effort for Jesus to endure the failings of his followers. To understand the nature of their failure, we have to recognize the phrase "faithless and twisted generation" as an echo of Deuteronomy 32, where Moses chides Israel for following foreign gods despite God's continued faithfulness.[1] Rather than "blowing his top" or impatiently snapping at the disciples, Jesus is lamenting the fact that they continue to waver between faith and faithlessness. But just as God does not give up on Old Testament Israel (see Deut. 32:43), Jesus continues to bear with the Twelve. Despite a string of failures (see Luke 9:45–46, 49–50, 54–55), he patiently instructs, rebukes, and corrects them. Their faith may waver, but Jesus' patience remains.

1. See especially Deut. 32:5, "a crooked and twisted generation," and Deut. 32:20, "a perverse generation, children in whom is no faithfulness."

### *Jesus' Response to Criticism and Rejection*

From his own disciples, Jesus faces persistent misunderstanding. From others, Jesus faces more active resistance—including murderous wrath (Luke 4:28–29), fury and secret plots against him (Luke 6:11; 11:53–54; 14:1), ridicule (Luke 16:14), and ultimately a decision to kill him (Luke 19:47; 20:19; 22:2). When contrasted to such hostility and violence, Jesus' self-restraint is remarkable. Though he is accused of blasphemy and Sabbath breaking, of being a "glutton and a drunkard, a friend of tax collectors and sinners" (Luke 7:34), and even of being in league with Satan (Luke 11:15), he answers his opponents with preached words rather than violent acts. For example, in Luke 13:14–17, when a synagogue ruler protests a Sabbath healing, Jesus responds with evidence and argument: first, even conservative Jewish leaders care for their animals on the Sabbath; second, the urgency of Jesus' mission means that a "daughter of Abraham" should not be left under Satan's power for even one more day (Luke 13:16). If such logic puts his adversaries "to shame" (Luke 13:17), it is because of the weight it carries, not because Jesus treats them with the same contempt they direct at him.

But is this the whole story? After all, Jesus' first words to the indignant synagogue ruler in Luke 13:15 are "You hypocrites!" In Luke 11:37–44, Jesus denounces the Pharisees in terms so strong that one of their scribes labels them insults; Jesus' response is an even more scathing denunciation of the scribes (Luke 11:45–52). Later, he drives merchants from the temple courts (Luke 19:45), engaging in what could be understood as a violent act. In addition, Jesus often employs graphic images of God's wrath and eternal punishment: "fear him who . . . has authority to cast into hell" (Luke 12:5); "the master of that servant . . . will cut him in pieces" ( Luke 12:46); "weeping and gnashing of teeth" (Luke 13:28); "torment . . . anguish" (Luke 16:23–25); "But as for these enemies of mine . . . slaughter them before me" (Luke 19:27). Do these facts somehow diminish Jesus' example as one who *patiently* endures hardship?

Several factors weigh against such a conclusion. First, Jesus stands in the tradition of the Hebrew prophets, who often used strong language and imagery to confront God's people in hopes that they would repent of sin and return to him. Second, when Jesus speaks of eternal punishment, he speaks not as an angry individual, but as the Son of Man whom God has appointed to carry out final judgment (Luke 9:26; 12:8–9, 40; 18:8; 21:27, 36)—a judgment that promotes mercy by removing from God's kingdom those who disturb its peace. Third, when Jesus denounces his opponents, it is not because he seeks revenge for personal slights against him, but because they are actively opposing God's purpose. For instance, as we saw in chapter 6, Jesus reserves the epithet "hypocrites" for those who appear to be well acquainted with God's purposes, but in fact only make the truth about him more obscure to those who most need mercy.[2]

Together, these factors help us to understand Jesus' expulsion of the merchants from the temple. Appearing to aid worshipers by selling items related to sacrifices, they are actually hindering God's purpose for the temple (Luke 19:46). Jesus' act is not a self-indulgent expression of rage by one who lacks proper authority, but a God-honoring condemnation of the corrupt temple leadership by Jerusalem's rightful King (see 19:38–40). Jesus' role as Messiah requires of him conduct that appears harsh,[3] yet he remains a model of restraint when contrasted with his adversaries. When he rebukes, they lie in wait (Luke 11:54); when he expels, they seek to destroy (Luke 19:47).

2. See Luke 6:42; 12:56; 13:15, and the similar use of "hypocrisy" at Luke 12:1.

3. For a discussion of how we might properly imitate this aspect of Jesus' character, see chapter 12, pp. 181–83.

## Compassion versus Retaliation

Just as Jesus calls us to respond with gentleness to those who reject, criticize, or offend us, he also makes it clear—perhaps uncomfortably clear—that we are to show mercy to those who seek to harm us:

> But I say to you who hear, Love your enemies, do good to those who hate you, bless those who curse you, pray for those who abuse you. To one who strikes you on the cheek, offer the other also, and from one who takes away your cloak do not withhold your tunic either. . . . and from one who takes away your goods do not demand them back. (Luke 6:27–30)

Our dealings with those who mistreat us ought to reflect the fact that our Father is "kind to the ungrateful and the evil. Be merciful, even as your Father is merciful" (Luke 6:35–36). It is not surprising, then, that Jesus, the Son of God, models compassion, rather than retaliation, toward his enemies.

### *Jesus' Compassion—and the Disciples' Anger*

Two passages in Luke portray Jesus as a model of non-retaliation by contrasting his example with that of the disciples. In Luke 9:52–56, Samaritan villagers refuse to welcome Jesus as he makes his way toward Jerusalem. James and John believe that such an affront calls for a drastic response: "Lord, do you want us to tell fire to come down from heaven and consume them?" (Luke 9:54). Luke's summary of Jesus' reply is powerful in its simplicity: "But he turned and rebuked them. And they went on to another village" (Luke 9:55–56).[4] The "Sons of Thunder" are silenced by Jesus' willingness to patiently endure rejection.

4. Some manuscripts of Luke's Gospel have longer versions of Luke 9:55–56. In both versions, the contrast between Jesus' example and his disciples' desire for vengeance is clear.

Luke 22 paints a similar picture. Seeing Judas and the armed officials who have come to arrest Jesus, his disciples ask, "Lord, shall we strike with the sword?" (Luke 22:49). Not waiting for an answer, one of them (Peter, according to John 18:10) cuts off the ear of the high priest's servant. Jesus shouts, "No more of this!" and—in an event recorded only by Luke—heals the servant's ear (see Luke 22:51). Not only does Jesus refuse to answer force with force, he compassionately heals one who has come to arrest him without cause. Jesus is as quick to show mercy as his followers are to show vengeance.

### *Jesus' Compassion and the Cross*

Luke's portrayal of Jesus as one who refuses to answer insult with insult, injury with injury, only intensifies after his arrest. The anger, contempt, and violence with which Jewish authorities (Luke 22:63–65), together with Herod and his troops (Luke 23:10–11), treat Jesus contrast sharply with the restraint he shows. His silence before Herod (Luke 23:9) reminds us of Isaiah 53:7: "He was oppressed, and he was afflicted, yet he opened not his mouth." Rather than curse the soldiers who nail him to the cross, Jesus prays, "Father, forgive them, for they know not what they do" (Luke 23:34).[5] And when Jesus is taunted by Jewish rulers, Roman soldiers, and one of the criminals crucified alongside him (Luke 23:35–39), he does not reply to their mockery. Rather than words of bitterness or vengeance for those who abuse him, Jesus has only words of comfort and assurance for the repentant criminal (Luke 23:43). Even to the end, Jesus models what he requires of us; patiently enduring the greatest hardships ever known, he remains merciful, even as his Father is merciful.

5. As most English translations point out, several early and reliable Greek manuscripts omit this sentence. For evidence that this prayer is original to Luke's Gospel and not a later addition, see David Crump, *Jesus the Intercessor: Prayer and Christology in Luke-Acts* (Tübingen: Mohr/Siebeck, 1992), 79–85.

## Conclusion: The Power for Endurance

Having surveyed Jesus' contentment, courage, gentleness, and compassion in the face of hardship, we have also encountered the power that motivates us to follow his example. As it turns out, it is the same power that enables daddies to carry heavy backpacks up steep hills in the hot sun—namely, love. Charlie and I didn't go hiking on the Ozark Trail to prove that we were tough or to atone for too many bowls of ice cream. We did it because we love our daughters, whose sixteenth birthdays we wanted to celebrate by taking them, and their younger sisters, on a backpacking trip. Because love motivated us, we were able not only to endure the challenges of the trail, but to find joy in the midst of the endurance. Hopefully, a closer look at the strength Jesus demonstrated as he experienced so many hardships has increased our love for him, and therefore our eagerness to imitate his patient endurance. The shape that imitation should take is the subject of our next chapter.

# 12

# Imitating Jesus' Patient Endurance of Hardship

EACH YEAR I SHARE a piece of advice with first-year seminary students who have little or no preaching experience: "Don't shoot yourself in the foot!" This is my way of suggesting that in the first few sermons they prepare for preaching classes, they should stay away from Scripture texts and topics that present challenges beyond the ordinary. One such topic is suffering. To speak biblical truth with pastoral sensitivity about a subject that has the potential to open deep wounds in the hearts of hearers is a challenge for even the most experienced preachers. As I write this chapter, I recognize how easy it would be for me to shoot myself in the foot—or worse, to stab readers in the heart.

Why, then, should I dare write, and you dare read, further? First, it is certain that each of us will endure suffering and hardship in this life. Turning away from hard questions will only leave us unprepared for life as disciples of Christ. Second, Scripture clearly teaches that we are to imitate Jesus' endurance of suffering. Even when it is difficult, careful thought about the practical realities of imitating him is part of our biblical duty. Third, the ultimate purpose of biblical teaching, even about Christlike endurance of hardship, is not to burden, crush, or overwhelm us, but to give us courage, strength, and hope. Many of us remember Scripture's insistence that "through many tribulations we must enter the kingdom of God" (Acts 14:22); fewer recall that Paul and Barnabas taught this truth in order to strengthen "the souls of the disciples, encouraging them to continue in the faith." It is with this same goal that I write and, I pray, you may read.

## Four Marks—and One Perspective

Based on our survey in chapter 11, we will focus in this chapter on four marks of Christlike endurance of hardship. However, it is essential that these four marks take their place in a balanced, biblical perspective on hardship and suffering. We begin by looking to Jesus' example to discover such a perspective.

Christian attitudes toward suffering and hardship can easily gravitate toward unhealthy extremes. On the one hand, some of us conclude that since suffering is a major feature of the Christian life, it must be good. As a result, we may try to cultivate indifference toward the enjoyment of good things, or we may adopt a stoic attitude toward pain. On the other hand, some of us take the reality of pain and suffering so seriously that we seek to avoid it altogether, even if this means ignoring the force of Jesus' words and example.

Note, however, that the pattern Jesus uses to summarize his own life—first suffering, then glory (Luke 24:26)—confronts both of these extremes. "First suffering" reminds us that we will never be able to completely avoid hardship as we pursue God's purposes in this world. If Jesus had ignored this truth, he might have agreed with Satan's logic in the wilderness, or he might have insisted on *his own* will at Gethsemane. "Then glory" reminds us that Jesus died and rose again to redeem us from suffering so that we might enjoy God's fullest blessings forever. If suffering were good in and of itself, Jesus would not have expressed his preference for letting the "cup" of God's wrath pass, and he would not have looked forward to Paradise as he hung on the cross. The "first suffering, then glory" pattern of Jesus' life calls us not to live at one end of the scale, but to combine great endurance of life's sorrows with intense enjoyment of God's blessings.

A third extreme perspective lumps all suffering together in one category. To appreciate the dangers of this perspective, consider three businessmen who represent three kinds of suffering. One faces financial insecurity and possible jail time because of unethical business practices. He suffers as a result of his own sinful choices. Another has lost his job because he refuses to lie about his company's corrupt financial practices in order to increase profits. The hardship he endures is a direct result of his faithfulness to Christ and the redemptive purposes of God's kingdom. A third has his entire business destroyed in a fire started by lightning. He suffers simply because he lives in a fallen world—a world where terrible things happen because God has cursed the sin of the human race as a whole.

Two significant problems result when we fail to distinguish these kinds of suffering. First, we can *excuse ourselves* by assuming that any suffering satisfies the demands of following Jesus. But a person may have lived a very hard life without ever having sacrificed anything "for the sake of the kingdom of God" (Luke 18:29). Our third businessman, for instance, might be tempted to say, "I've endured my hardship; now I can take it easy and start enjoying my glory!" But his suffering, while painful and extremely trying, doesn't show us whether he is ready to endure hardship that results from faithfulness to Christ. Second, we can *blame others* by assuming that suffering reflects sinfulness. Subtly, we can treat anyone who endures misfortune as though it were deserved: "Homeless people are probably lazy. He has health problems because he eats too much." Such logic, rejected by Jesus in Luke 13:1–5 ("Do you think that these . . . were worse sinners . . . because they suffered in this way? No, I tell you. . . ."), would presume that our second and third businessmen were guilty, just like the first.

How does Jesus' example of patient endurance relate to these three kinds of suffering? It is clear that Jesus never suffered because of his own sin or foolishness. But if Jesus could respond with patience when condemned for sins he never committed, how much more should we patiently endure the consequences of the wrong we have done? Many of the principles in this chapter will thus apply to our first businessman, though his circumstances least resemble those of Jesus. Similarly, the principles we learn here apply to our third businessman; though Jesus' own suffering is primarily a result of his faithfulness to God, his example teaches us how to respond to any difficult circumstance. For this reason, we are called to follow in his footsteps even when the lines among our three categories are blurred. Most of us are a mixture of suffering sinner, suffering saint, and suffering victim, but all of us may learn from the example of Jesus.[1]

## The First Mark: Steady under Pressure

With this framework in place, we may now identify four marks of Christlike endurance. These marks are not intended to exhaust every aspect of Jesus' response to hardship, but to collect the major themes surveyed in chapter 11 under headings that provide practical focus for our imitation of Jesus' example. If we are to patiently endure hardship as Jesus did, we must be people who are: (1) steady under pressure, (2) slow to anger, (3) quick to mercy, and (4) full of joy. As we shall now see, being steady under pressure means facing our fears, and taking a long-term perspective on suffering.

1. See Michael Emlet, *CrossTalk: Where Life and Scripture Meet* (Greensboro, NC: New Growth Press, 2009), who portrays Christians as sufferers, sinners, and saints.

### *Facing Our Fears*

To imitate Jesus' courage, we must learn to remain steady in the face of those things that are most likely to intimidate us. I remember feeling intimidated when my wife, Tricia, and I had to make a final commitment to move to Scotland for me to study at the University of Aberdeen. I confided to Dr. Phil Long, one of my seminary professors, that I was scared of doing something foolish. He replied, "Jimmy, the only foolish thing is to know the will of God and fail to do it." Even when scriptural principles, the counsel of others, and the honest evaluation of our gifts, desires, and circumstances allow us to clearly discern a vocational direction or ministry priority, we can be intimidated by what it might cost us, by the fear of appearing foolish, or by the possibility of failure. The same applies to moral choices, as when we seek to maintain wise, scriptural standards regarding finances in a culture that is increasingly irresponsible and materialistic. From Jesus' example we learn to pursue God's will courageously, no matter what the consequences.

Two other forms of intimidation deserve mention. First, we can be intimidated by the scale of tasks that lie before us: the recovering alcoholic is staggered by the thought of remaining sober for the rest of his life; many fathers tremble at the thought of leading family worship on a consistent basis; the schoolteacher weeps to know that for every abused child she helps, dozens of others pass through her classes every day. Second, we can be intimidated by our own history of sin and spiritual weakness. Scripture is silent about whether Jesus faced the first of these fears, and being sinless he never faced the second. But we know that he did face the one thing that makes every other fear pale in comparison—namely, the wrath of God, which he endured at the cross. Since our Savior faced this fear so that we will never have to, surely we are strengthened to face courageously every lesser fear as well.

### *A Long-Term Perspective*

Being steady under pressure also means making steady progress toward goals set by our Father and his Son, not by our own desires for comfort and control. Therefore we have to reject what we might call the sprinter's approach to enduring hardship—the view that if we *occasionally* endure *intense* periods of difficulty, then we are growing in Christlikeness. In Luke's Gospel, Jesus' patient endurance is not an occasional departure from a more comfortable norm; rather, it is the overall trajectory of his life. Thus, while Jesus can avoid particular kinds of suffering at particular moments—for instance, walking away from a murderous mob in Nazareth (Luke 4:29–30) or leaving Herod's territory after learning that Herod wants to kill him (Luke 13:31–33)—he consistently endures the suffering to which his Father calls him. This is what we might call the marathoner's perspective: if we *consistently* pursue our Father's purposes, bearing *over time* whatever hardship this may entail, then we are following the example of Christ.

## The Second Mark: Slow to Anger

Oil and water don't mix. Because the same can be said of anger and patience, we must be people who are slow to anger if we are to imitate Jesus' patient endurance of hardship.

### *Anger against God*

In chapter 11, we observed repeatedly Jesus' contentment with doing God's will. A major barrier to such contentment for us is anger against God, which often flows from (1) frustration with the difficult circumstances of our lives, (2) bitterness at God's failure to bless us as we feel we deserve, or (3) envy at how he has blessed others. Ultimately, these three share the faulty assumption that *greater proximity merits greater prosperity*—that is, the closer we are to God and his purposes, the fewer difficulties we should have to endure. We hear such logic from Satan in the wilderness (Luke 4:1–13) and from those who mock Jesus during his crucifixion (Luke 23:35–39). It is also evident in the older brother of Luke 15:25–30, who becomes angry with his father when he experiences less blessing than he thinks he deserves. The example of Jesus severs the root of such logic, and of the anger it feeds. If the Son of God, with whom the Father is "well pleased" (Luke 3:22), endures greater suffering than any person ever has or will, then we must not be so quick to connect outward circumstances with the presence or absence of God's approval. Even when our circumstances are at their worst, God is not a fit object for our anger, but a loving Father with whom we can share our deepest struggles (Luke 22:42) and whose hands can be trusted to keep us safely (Luke 23:46).

### *Anger against People*

Christlike patience in the face of hardship requires that we battle not only our anger against God, but also our anger against people. This is not to say that all anger is sinful, or that there are no godly ways to express anger.[2] However, Jesus exemplifies forgiveness, patience, and gentleness in situations where we are most likely to sinfully indulge our anger, bitterness, and harshness. Being like him means becoming a person who is slow to anger against the following kinds of people:

- *Those who betray and deny us*: Perhaps none of us will be arrested on false charges because of a friend like Judas, or denied three times in the same night by a friend like Peter. But at some point all of us will be exposed to criticism, ridicule, or loss by those we trust. Like Jesus, we are free

2. For further discussion, see pp. 168–79 of chapter 11, and pp. 181–83 below.

to acknowledge the pain of such betrayal (recall Luke 22:21, 48). And, like Jesus, we are called to exercise restraint rather than giving full vent to our anger. As Jesus prayed for Peter (Luke 22:32), we are even called to pray for such people, and to hold out hope for future reconciliation. Judas's example reminds us that there may be situations where such reconciliation is impossible, but our sinful tendency to escalate conflict suggests that we should err on the side of mercy.

- *Those who criticize, reject, or seek to harm us*: Here the greater-to-lesser logic of imitation is in full force. If Jesus demonstrated gentleness and restraint when he was criticized for doing God's will, how much more should we be willing to bear insult and injury in lesser matters? And if Jesus could pray for the soldiers who crucified him (Luke 23:34), how much more are we called to treat with mercy those who harm us in less serious ways? Jesus' example does not require that every person who is abused or physically attacked should passively endure harm[3]—but it does challenge us to become the kind of people who are (1) ready to endure great pain where doing so will multiply God's mercy in a fallen world and (2) ready to show mercy to those who sin against us.
- *People who sin against us or disappoint us, even repeatedly*: Repeat offenders and those who chronically fail to meet our expectations are frequently victims of our anger. Yet Jesus dealt mercifully with Peter, despite Peter's threefold denial of him, and he remained patient with his disciples despite their persistent failures. In each case he did confront sin and correct misunderstanding, but with a combination of firmness, clarity, and mercy rather than

3. Both Jesus and Paul were ready to endure suffering where this would advance God's redemptive purpose, and to avoid suffering that threatened to hinder that purpose (see Luke 4:29–30; Acts 9:23–25; 14:5–6; 17:5–14; 20:3; 22:22–29; 25:1–12). Clearly, great wisdom is required to discern the difference.

wrath. According to Jesus' example, forgiveness does not mean ignoring sin; rather, it means that we do not require others to pay a price for sins that have been forgiven.

- *People who tell the truth about us in unflattering ways*: Many criticisms of Jesus did contain an aspect of the truth. He may not have been a glutton and a drunkard, but it is true that he was a friend of, and shared table fellowship with, tax collectors and sinners! We often grow angry when others misrepresent us by telling partial truths, or even when they tell the truth about sinful or foolish things we have done. Jesus' example calls us to endure such hardship with patience, being slow to anger even in situations where sin tells us to do otherwise.

### *Hard Words, Not Humiliating*

Anyone who has been in a position of authority—as a parent, a teacher, an employer, a coach—knows how easy it is to cross the line from *correcting* someone to *belittling* them. "You didn't do what you were told" easily becomes, "You never listen, you never get anything right, and you make me *sick*!" To endure hardship patiently as Jesus did, we must learn from him how to speak hard words that are not angry, humiliating words.

As we saw in chapter 11, Jesus knew how to speak hard words. He spoke of the reality of hell, he called spiritual leaders who peddled dangerous doctrine "hypocrites," and he spoke truth about God and his purposes in ways that made many people uncomfortable. What we did not see was any evidence that Jesus spoke hard words out of bitterness or with a desire to "get even" with his critics. Three principles will guide us as we imitate Jesus' example:

- *The hardest words are for those who are a danger to others, not those who are a frustration to us.* Jesus' harshest denunciations were reserved for religious leaders with potential to mislead many others. He also had hard things to say about idols such as money and pride, which have potential to ensnare many. Like him, we are called to speak hard words when they will correct and protect, not when they will bring us personal satisfaction or score a victory for "our side."

- *Even hard words have a merciful purpose*. As the parable of the prodigal son ends, the older brother is outside the banquet and the father has gone out to plead with him—but we are not told how the older brother responds to his father's pleading (Luke 15:25–32). The parable therefore serves as an open call for Jesus' opponents (see Luke 15:2) to repent and be reconciled to God. When we must speak hard words of correction to others, we must ask whether we are similarly open to an outcome of reconciliation; will we delight in others' change and growth, or are we secretly rejoicing in their failure?
- *"Fault-finding" is crossing the line*. In Luke 11:1, one of Jesus' disciples says, "Lord, teach us to pray." What if, instead of teaching the Lord's Prayer, Jesus had responded with fault-finding and criticism? "What a joke! You haven't listened to anything else I've ever tried to teach you—so why should I even bother?!" Thankfully, Jesus responds by patiently instructing his disciples, despite their consistent failures. Fault-finding is a form of humiliating speech, and we must avoid it if we are to grow in likeness to Jesus.

### *Reorienting Our Outrage*

Underlying the things we have said to this point about being slow to anger is another aspect of Christ's example—namely, the orientation of his outrage. You and I tend to be extremely sensitive to personal slights, responding with anger when our sense of worth or well-being is threatened. By contrast, Jesus responds most intensely when God's honor and purposes are undermined (as at Luke 11:42–52; 19:45–46) or when people in need are hindered from enjoying God's mercy (as at Luke 9:41; 13:14–17). Put another way, Jesus' outrage has an "upward" and "outward" orientation, whereas sin causes our outrage to have an "inward" orientation. To patiently endure hardship, we must be slow to anger. Yet this will be possible only when our hearts are transformed in such a way that we take more offense when God and neighbor fail to receive the love they are due than when we ourselves are dishonored or mistreated.

## The Third Mark: Quick to Mercy

As we have just seen, imitating Christ's patient endurance of hardship requires a double negative: we must be *slow* to *anger*. But there is a corresponding double positive: as people who are growing in Christlikeness, we must be *quick* to *mercy*. While chapter 8 dealt with what it means to imitate Jesus' passion for others' good, here we will focus on the connection between patient endurance of hardship and extending mercy to those in need.

### *Mercy to the Most Needy*

Jesus' insistence on extending God's mercy to those in need consistently draws the ire of leaders who disagree with him, teaching us that we too must be prepared to endure hardship, and even opposition, in the course of multiplying God's mercy. The following scenarios come to mind:

- A student once told me of his experience living in low-income housing. He was eventually asked to stop inviting neighboring children to attend church with him, for fear that children of church members might get lice.

- On a mission trip in an urban area, a team I was serving with met with many disapproving comments. Our efforts to clean the home of a woman who could not afford garbage service were disturbing the nests of rats, mice, and roaches, which were looking for shelter in her neighbors' homes.

Do I want my children to get lice, or my home to be infested with rats? Honestly, no. But the truth is that all too often, I don't really want needy people to receive mercy, either. And if faced with a choice, it is much easier to stop showing mercy than to pay a price to do so.

Jesus calls us to a path that is more demanding, in that it exposes us to three kinds of costs. First, a commitment to show mercy to those in need exposes us to criticism. Among other things, we may be called unfair ("Why are you helping this person, and not that one? Why not everybody?"), incompetent ("There's a better way to do this."), or even uncommitted ("What you're doing is good, but why aren't you doing more?"). Second, such a commitment means that we must give up many of our resources such as time, money, energy—and, in some circumstances, health and safety. Third, showing mercy to those in need means we must pay the price of imaginative discernment. That is, we must invest time and effort in discerning when God is calling us to help neighbors in need, and in creatively determining how to meet their needs so that God's mercy is maximized. Such imaginative discernment might have prompted my inner-city mission team to ask questions like, "Where will all these rats go when we move this garbage? Would it be helpful to contact an exterminator? What if we gave two or three mousetraps to each neighbor, then explained to them what we are doing—and in whose Name we are doing it?" And imaginative discernment might have prompted the neighbors to ask, "Why does the lady next door never put a garbage can out on collection day?" Asking questions like these generally puts us on a path that leads to some costly demonstration of mercy—a path that should feel familiar to those who follow in the footsteps of Jesus.

### *Mercy to the Least Worthy*

Imitating Jesus means loving the "tax collectors and sinners" of our day, those considered least worthy of love from God, from the church, even from society—and bearing whatever hardship accompanies our fellowship with them.

Sometimes the hardship is criticism and rejection, and sometimes it is more significant. On a missionary assignment in South Africa, a friend of mine had grown weary of preaching the gospel to the people in his neighborhood. It was unsafe for him to walk alone, so he had to buy a car; but every time he parked at a business, a gang member would approach to ask for protection money to ensure that no "accidents" would happen while the car was unattended. One day, in frustration, my friend complained to a more experienced missionary, "I'm giving up so much to help these people—and I'm sick of it! How am I supposed to love people like this?" His mentor replied, "Just remember: Jesus had to stoop a lot further to love you than you will ever have to stoop to love them." Christ was quick to show mercy to the "least worthy"—including us. Remembering this changes us, making us quick to mercy as well.

### *Quick Mercy to Slow Learners*

As we noted in chapter 11, Jesus is patient with his disciples, though they persistently fail to show the kind of spiritual maturity he desires. Like him, we must be quick to show mercy to those who are slow to learn. Parents will quickly understand how challenging this is! When our children make foolish choices, as though they've forgotten everything we ever tried to teach them about responsibility, respect for authority, or love for Christ, we experience a mixture of sadness, fear, and frustration. While we may be tempted to nurse our resentment, Jesus' example teaches us that we must be quick to show mercy to our children—quick to seek reconciliation, quick to forgive, quick to reassure them of our love, and quick to support them as they face the consequences of whatever they may have done. The same applies to anyone in an authority role. When those we are training, nurturing, coaching, and mentoring need more time to grow, we are called to provide it patiently.

Imagine, then, a father who says to his son, "I need you to clean up the front yard." The son may not yet understand that "clean up" includes weeding the flower beds. And because he's still learning and growing, his notion of a thorough job is not what it should be. His father, instead of being quick to criticize, is called by the example of Jesus to be quick to show mercy. That means being quick to ask forgiveness for any harsh words already spoken, quick to offer encouragement for what has been done well—and quick to remember that shaping a child's heart is worth the time and effort required.

## The Fourth Mark: Full of Joy

What will make us steady under pressure, slow to anger, and quick to mercy? What is the spring from which the marks of such character will flow? A fourth mark, being full of joy, serves not only as an additional indicator that we are growing as imitators of Christ, but also as a source of power that sustains our growth.

### *Joy in God's Promises*

According to Hebrews 12:2, Jesus endured the cross "for the joy that was set before him." Luke's Gospel presents us with a similar picture. On multiple occasions, Jesus speaks of his suffering and death together with his coming glory, including both his resurrection (Luke 9:22; 18:31–33; 24:26, 46) and his triumphant return as the glorious Son of Man (Luke 17:24–25; see also 22:69). Similarly, Jesus anticipates the blessings of "Paradise" even as he hangs on the cross (Luke 23:43). The implication is that God's promises of future glory motivate and strengthen Jesus to endure hardship.

For us the implication is clear: to endure like Jesus, we must cling to the same hope that he did. The promises that God will give us joy in his presence when we die, and that he will one day give us resurrection bodies, delivering us and all of creation from every effect of sin's curse—these are our strength when facing hardship of any kind. Knowing that we will share in the same resurrection life that Jesus already enjoys gives us hope as we seek to imitate his patient endurance.

### *Joy in God's Character*

Implied in what we have just said is a truth that seems obvious, but is profound in its significance. If Jesus finds joy, hope, and strength in his Father's promises, then he must believe that his Father is trustworthy and good. He is not the kind of God who makes a promise and fails to keep it. Nor is he the kind of Father who offers a good gift, and cruelly substitutes something painful in its place (Luke 11:11–13). When Jesus speaks of God as "Father," he reveals to us another source of strength—namely, confidence that God is able and willing to give every good thing that he promises. This is especially apparent in the closing chapters of Luke, where Jesus three times addresses God as Father: "Father, if you are willing" (Luke 22:42); "Father, forgive them" (Luke 23:34); "Father, into your hands" (Luke 23:46). Even to the end, when every circumstance surrounding his death says otherwise, the Son knows the Father to be merciful and faithful. Only with such a Father to love us can we endure hardship as patiently and courageously as the Son.

## Conclusion: From Oriented to Enabled

In chapter 4, we addressed the need for a simple, practical approach to imitating Christ in our daily lives. We have now summarized such an approach using four major principles: passion for the glory of God; passion for the good of others; willing denial of self; and patient endurance of hardship. In chapters 5–12, we have seen how each of these traits characterized the life of Jesus, and what it might mean for us to orient our own lives by these same principles. To pick up on an image we used earlier, we are like a hiker equipped with a compass. Even though it is marked with only four cardinal directions, he can use it to orient himself no matter where he is. He is equipped with a simple tool, but ready to negotiate any number of complex tasks.

Yet, as any experienced hiker would tell us, being able to find your way is only half the battle. On the Ozark Trail with our daughters (see chapter 11), my friend Charlie and I ran into a large group of half-prepared backpackers. They had plenty of maps and compasses, but very little water. They knew where they wanted to go, and they had plenty of directions for getting there. But in the mountains, in the hot sun, water is fuel—and their tanks were empty. We left them on the mountainside with sad news: at the bottom of the mountain they would find plenty of water, but only after a needlessly wearying hike down. We do not want to be half-prepared imitators of Christ, knowing exactly what we need to do, but having no source of strength to do it. This chapter's comments on joy point us to one of the resources that will sustain our growth in Christlikeness—but this is only one of many life-giving streams that flow through Luke's Gospel. In our next chapter, we therefore seek a fuller answer to a crucial question: According to Luke's Gospel, what is the fuel that gives us strength to follow in the footsteps of Christ? What sources of power will enable us to carry out all the challenges of imitating our Savior?

# 13

# Fuel and Fire: How Real People Grow as Imitators of Christ

"I WANNA BE LIKE MIKE." With that refrain as its soundtrack, the old commercial featured footage of Michael Jordan, the greatest basketball player of his generation, interwoven with clips of children playing in games of their own. The contrast raised a question: by what means does an average kid come to resemble a superstar athlete? A final screen drove home the answer: "Be like Mike. Drink Gatorade." Even if we doubt whether a sports drink could give us Jordanesque talent, we can still appreciate the distinction on which the commercial's logic turned: if you want the *marks* of "Mike-likeness" on the court—agility and athleticism, a seeming ability to defy gravity, and a competitive drive that refuses to stop—then you need to employ the proper *means* for becoming "like Mike."

In chapters 5–12 of our study, we have examined the marks of Christlikeness. We have asked the question, "In what ways should Christians be like Jesus?," and found in Luke's Gospel a fourfold response: (1) in our passion for the glory of God, (2) in our passion for the good of others, (3) in our willing denial of self, and (4) in our patient endurance of hardship. Now, however, we must give focused attention to the *means* of Christlikeness, the things that will sustain us, change us, and enable us to grow as imitators of Christ in these four areas. As we turn once more to Luke's Gospel, we will encounter five such means:

- The power of the Holy Spirit
- The triad of repentance, forgiveness, and joy
- A pattern in which indicatives empower imperatives
- Warnings of judgment and the consequences of sin
- Faith and prayer

To provide a proper framework for understanding these means, we must first identify two profoundly flawed approaches to spiritual growth in general, and therefore to growth in Christlikeness.

## Avoiding Easy Ways Out

Two unbalanced, but not uncommon, approaches to spiritual growth are *passivism* and *moralism*. The first assumes that spiritual growth depends entirely on God, involving little or no human effort, while the second views such growth as entirely a product of human effort, a simple matter of Christians doing what we are told. Both are easy ways out, one absolving us of our responsibility to pursue growth, and the other eliminating the need to depend on God's transforming grace. Two basic truths from Luke's Gospel establish a framework that is not only more balanced, but more faithful to Scripture.

First, Luke's Gospel teaches us that *sustained, intense effort is a necessary component of spiritual growth*. A few themes from Jesus' teaching illustrate the point:

- *Discipleship demands radical commitment.* Disciples must deny themselves and take up their crosses daily, renouncing all that they have to follow Jesus (Luke 9:23; 14:26–27, 33). "No one who puts his hand to the plow and looks back is fit for the kingdom of God," says Jesus (Luke 9:62).
- *Discipleship demands constant vigilance.* Jesus repeatedly calls his disciples to "take care" (Luke 8:18; 12:15), "beware/be on guard" (Luke 12:1, 15), "pay attention to yourselves" (Luke 17:3), and "watch yourselves" (Luke 21:34). As we await his return we must "stay awake at all times" (Luke 21:36), "dressed for action" with our "lamps burning" (Luke 12:35).
- *Discipleship demands persistent effort.* It is not enough to "hear the word"; we must "hold it fast," bearing fruit "with patience" (Luke 8:13, 15). Jesus says the door to his house is narrow, so that we enter not casually but through striving (Luke 13:24–25).
- *Discipleship demands exacting obedience.* Jesus' disciples must put his words into practice (Luke 6:46–49), even when their demands are extreme (Luke 6:27–36). Indeed, the more we know of Jesus, the greater our obligation to obey (Luke 12:48).

Scripture sets each of these demands in the larger context of God's gracious provision to us through Jesus; yet it would be a mistake to emphasize God's provision in a way that weakens such demands. Whatever we conclude about the means by which we grow as imitators of Christ, significant human effort must be a part—never the whole, but certainly a part—of our approach.

Second, Luke's Gospel teaches us that *knowledge of our duty is not a sufficient condition for spiritual growth*. In addition to knowing what is required of us, we need a spiritual transformation that will make us willing and able to do our duty. Consider three examples:

- *Trees, fruit, and foundations (Luke 6:43–49)*: Jesus concludes the Sermon on the Plain with the image of a man building a house with no foundation, reminding us that not everyone who hears his words will put them into practice. The preceding images—good fruit coming from good trees, not from bad trees or thorn bushes—indicate that right response to Jesus requires not only hearing his teaching, but transformation of the heart.
- *The rich ruler (Luke 18:18–23)*: Here Jesus encounters a wealthy Jewish official who desires eternal life. Yet when Jesus points out the "one thing" the official lacks—giving up his possessions to follow Jesus—the official refuses. The ruler hears his duty from Jesus himself, but is unwilling to do it, because his heart is still gripped by the idol of wealth.
- *Forgiveness and faith (Luke 17:3–6)*: When Jesus requires willingness to forgive those who sin against us, even seven times in the same day, the apostles cry out, "Increase our faith!" (Luke 17:5). Even Jesus' closest followers understand that the obedience he requires is not possible on the basis of human strength alone.

In light of these emphases, we see that spiritual growth, and growth in Christlikeness, must involve dependence on God to transform us through his power and mercy—doing for us what we could never do for ourselves. With these two basic starting points in place—the necessity of human effort, and the necessity of divine transformation—we may now survey five themes from Luke's Gospel that show us how such transformation occurs, and how such effort is sustained.

## The Power of the Holy Spirit

How can we become more like Jesus in our character and conduct? Luke's portrayal of Jesus' life and ministry suggests that our answer to this question should begin with an emphasis on the power of the Holy Spirit. The very origin of Jesus' life as a human is the result of the Spirit's work (Luke 1:35), and it is the Spirit, descending at Jesus' baptism, who empowers God's Servant-Son for his mission (Luke 3:21–22). Since Jesus enters his wilderness temptation "full of the Holy Spirit" and "led by the Spirit" (Luke 4:1), we may infer that the Spirit gives Jesus strength to resist temptation and to fulfill his calling as the faithful, obedient second Adam. Similarly, Jesus begins his public ministry "in the power of the Spirit" (Luke 4:14), who has anointed him to extend God's mercies to the poor, the captive, the blind, and the oppressed (Luke 4:18). Jesus' life, characterized by devotion to God and his purposes rather than to sin and self, is the paradigm for all of God's people. And the power behind that life is the Holy Spirit.

It should encourage us, then, to know that the same power is at work in all who trust Jesus. As John the Baptist promised, Jesus has baptized us with the Holy Spirit (Luke 3:16; Acts 1:5; 11:16). According to Acts, this Spirit baptism represents the culmination of a sequence of events: Jesus is crucified, resurrected, and exalted to God's right hand; here he receives from his Father "the promise of the Holy Spirit"; he then pours out the Spirit on the church (Acts 2:32–33; 5:30–32). Along with the Spirit, Jesus gives his people the gifts of repentance and the forgiveness of sins (Acts 2:38; 5:31). By the Spirit's power our resistance to God melts into repentance, our sins are cleansed, and we are given strength for renewed life. In short, the Spirit fuels our growth in every aspect of godliness, including likeness to Christ.

Three things remain to be said about the Spirit's work in our lives according to Luke and Acts. First, one of the primary means by which the Spirit works is God's revealed truth. It is thus no surprise that Jesus, "full of the Spirit," constantly returns to Scripture when resisting Satan in the wilderness (Luke 4:1–13), nor that Acts so frequently links the Spirit to the Word of God, whether written (Acts 1:16; 4:25; 28:25) or proclaimed (Acts 4:31; 13:48–52). Practically, then, growth as imitators of Christ will require immersion in Scripture, a point to which we will return in our next chapter. Second, Luke has much to say, especially in Acts, about how the Spirit equips God's people for worldwide witness to the redeeming work accomplished through Jesus.[1] By implication, as we grow in likeness to Christ we will increasingly long to extend the blessings of salvation to the world by the Spirit's power. Finally, we should note Luke's assumption that when the exalted Jesus pours out the Spirit on us, he does not diminish his own share of resurrection life and power. Because Jesus possesses the Spirit in infinite measure, and shares that same Spirit with us, we know that we have access to all the divine power needed to move us from patterns of sin and failure to patterns of Christlike holiness and love.[2]

## Repentance, Forgiveness, and Joy

Closely related to the power of the Holy Spirit is a chain of cause and effect that pervades Luke's Gospel: the grace of the gospel prompts repentance, which is accompanied by forgiveness of sins; this produces joy, which fuels love; such love in turn expresses itself in complete devotion and radical obedience to God and to his Son. Since the imitation of Christ demands such devotion, the triad of repentance, forgiveness,

1. This is particularly emphasized in Acts 2, where we learn that all of God's people are being empowered to attest to the "mighty works of God" (Acts 2:11).

2. For an excellent overview of Scripture's teaching about the Holy Spirit, see John D. Harvey, *Anointed with the Spirit and Power: The Holy Spirit's Empowering Presence*, Explorations in Biblical Theology (Phillipsburg, NJ: P&R Publishing, 2008).

and joy must be among the means by which Christlikeness is produced in our lives.

Jesus often emphasizes this pattern in disputes with those who object to his association with sinners, and nowhere more clearly than in Luke 7:36–50. When Simon the Pharisee criticizes Jesus for allowing a sinful woman to anoint his feet, Jesus tells a short parable about a moneylender and two debtors to demonstrate that forgiveness should prompt love (Luke 7:41–42). Jesus goes on to contrast the woman's lavish expressions of love with Simon's failure to show even basic gestures of respect for an honored guest (Luke 7:44–46), and he offers this conclusion: "Therefore I tell you, her sins which are many, are forgiven—for she loved much. But he who is forgiven little, loves little" (Luke 7:48).[3] Those who sense no need for forgiveness will never know the joy that fuels love. But those who know the enormity of their debt before God delight in his forgiveness, and therefore devote themselves to him. There is no question that the imitation of Christ calls for extravagant obedience; similarly, there can be no question that the desire for such obedience must be fueled by a repentant, joyful response to the mercy of God.

This conclusion is confirmed in Luke 15. When Pharisees and scribes grumble that Jesus welcomes tax collectors and sinners (Luke 15:2), they show that they are not his imitators, for while Jesus rejoices that sinners are being restored to God through repentance, his critics do just the opposite! It is instructive, then, to see how Jesus attempts to change their perspective, and thus their practice. His strategy is not simply to say, "You need to be more like me, so start rejoicing when sinners repent!" Rather, Jesus tells parables that reveal the gracious character of God—he is the shepherd who goes after one lost sheep, the woman who

3. The logic of Jesus' parable, in which forgiveness produces love, makes it clear that the woman's love is a *response to* the forgiveness of her sins, not the *cause of* that forgiveness. The implication is that she has previously embraced Jesus' promises of forgiveness.

searches intently for her lost coin, the father who celebrates the return of a rebellious son. But these parables include a challenge: those who are "righteous" in their own eyes and "need no repentance" (Luke 15:7), who would rather recite their own record of obedience than participate in the heavenly Father's joy-giving rescue of sinners (Luke 15:29–30), will never experience God's gracious character. Without repentance, we can never have anything to do with God's purposes. But with repentance comes a forgiveness so complete, so beyond our comprehension, that we delight, as Jesus delights, to do our Father's will.

But can joy truly enable obedience? If the parables of Luke 15 left any doubt, the account of Zacchaeus in Luke 19:1–10 does not. While the crowds grumble at Jesus' association with a sinner, Zacchaeus receives Jesus "joyfully" (Luke 19:6). Zacchaeus then renounces his idolatrous pursuit of wealth, committing to give half of his goods to the poor and to make restitution to those he has defrauded (Luke 19:8). When Jesus seeks and saves "the lost" (Luke 19:10), the lost respond with joy and with costly obedience—thus confirming the transforming power of God's mercy. Luke never says so explicitly, but the pattern is undeniable: our efforts at imitating Jesus must be fueled by the repentance, forgiveness, and joy that accompany the salvation he brings.

## Indicatives Empowering Imperatives

Forgiveness produces joyful love for God. The promises of the gospel prompt repentance. These are specific instances of a broader dynamic that characterizes Luke's Gospel (and, for that matter, all of Scripture), one in which indicatives empower imperatives. Here we are borrowing grammatical terms to express a theological truth. Grammatically speaking, verbs in the indicative mood are those which make statements and assertions ("*I want* you to get better."); verbs in the imperative mood are those which issue commands ("So *take* your medicine!"). Applied to Scripture, indicatives are truths about God's character, actions, or promises, and imperatives are commands, prohibitions, duties, or obligations. To say that indicatives empower imperatives, then, is to say we find strength for obedience—including the imitation of Christ—in truths about God, grace, and the gospel.

While we need to feel the full force of the imperatives that Jesus issues in Luke's Gospel, we need also to notice how they are supported by indicatives. The following themes illustrate the indicative-imperative relationship:

- *Jesus' promises of God's care strengthen our devotion to God's purposes.* Jesus calls us to seek God's kingdom, freeing us from anxiety by reminding us (1) that God knows our needs; (2) that God himself will feed and clothe us; and (3) that God is pleased to give us his kingdom, with all of its treasures (Luke 12:22–34). Similarly, the Beatitudes of Luke 6:20–23 enable the endurance of various hardships through promises of blessing.
- *Jesus' promises of his own presence and provision strengthen us for cross-bearing and self-denial.* In Luke 9:20–26 and Luke 14:25–33, the command to deny ourselves and take up a cross is accompanied by several powerful motivations: (1) Jesus, the Messiah, will suffer and be raised for us; (2) Jesus goes with us/before us, because we are following him; (3) through allegiance to Jesus we will ultimately save our lives, sharing in his glory when he returns. The weight of these motivations suggests that we are unable to meet Jesus' demands unless we find strength in what he promises and provides.
- *Jesus' promises of wisdom and salvation empower us to endure persecution without anxiety.* Twice Jesus instructs his disciples not to worry about how to defend themselves in

times of persecution. In Luke 12:4–12 and Luke 21:12–19, he grounds this requirement in various promises: (1) Jesus/the Holy Spirit will give us wisdom and the words to say to our accusers; (2) if we acknowledge Jesus before men, he will acknowledge us when he returns in judgment; (3) there is no need to fear what human opponents can do to us, because only God can condemn us eternally—and he values us so much that not even a hair of our heads will perish.

- *The hope of Jesus' return motivates perseverance.* While many will faint with fear in the days of distress that precede Jesus' return, we who trust him can lift our heads, "because [our] redemption is drawing near" (Luke 21:28). Likewise, servants who find it hard to stay awake, alert, and ready to do their Master's bidding should find strength in the promise that when he comes he will "dress himself for service" and serve them a feast (Luke 12:35–37).
- *Knowledge of God's character, and of Jesus' character, strengthens us for radical obedience.* Knowing that God is a righteous judge who will answer our cries for justice should motivate us "always to pray and not lose heart" (Luke 18:1–8). By contrast, viewing Jesus as "severe" and likely to exploit others makes us unwilling to put forth effort and risk in serving him (Luke 19:11–27). More explicitly related to imitation, Jesus appeals to our Father's merciful character as a motive for loving our enemies (Luke 6:35–36), and he appeals to his own character ("I am among you as the one who serves," Luke 22:27) when calling us to reject worldly patterns of greatness.

Based on these themes, we may assume that strength for imitating Christ will be rooted in the promises Jesus makes to us, the blessings he secures for us, and the character of God he reveals to us.

Of course, the place where God's character, blessings, and promises are climactically displayed is the crucifixion and resurrection of Jesus, which together form the most powerful indicative of Luke's Gospel. The crucifixion-resurrection pattern strengthens us to seek spiritual growth by assuring us that through Christ God has fully pardoned our sins, and is now working powerfully to reverse all the effects of sin's curse. With the indicatives of Jesus' cross and empty tomb as our anchor, we need not fear facing any imperative—even one as demanding as imitating him.

## The Powerful Discipline of Warnings

The preceding sections have focused mainly on positive sources of strength and motivation for obedience. Yet Jesus' teaching also contains many warnings of the dire consequences that accompany refusal to embrace him and his teaching. These warnings fall into two major categories. First, Jesus frequently refers to future judgment, when those who refuse to repent and to embrace the salvation God offers in his Son will experience divine punishment.[4] Second, Jesus often warns against the seductive power of idols, which secure our affection by promising great gain in the present, only to leave us spiritually destitute. The idols that receive special attention in Luke are wealth (Luke 12:13–21; 16:14–15), desire for status (Luke 14:7–11), fear of man that leads to denial of Jesus (Luke 9:26; 12:8–9), and self-righteousness that leads to despising of others (Luke 18:9–14).

4. Occasionally in Luke, Jesus refers to an individual's judgment at the moment of death (Luke 12:13–21; 16:19–31), but more often he speaks of a final, cosmic judgment that accompanies his second coming (for example, Luke 10:13–15; 11:29–32; 12:41–48; 13:1–9, 23–30; 17:22–37). The Westminster Confession of Faith 32.1 treats the former ("hell") as an anticipation of the latter ("the judgment of the great day").

Jesus' warnings could give the impression that the primary power for obedience is fear. However, three factors argue against this conclusion. First, many of these warnings occur in contexts that offer positive promises as well. In one striking example, Jesus tells us to "fear him [God] who . . . has authority to cast into hell," then goes on to say, "Fear not; you are of more value [to God] than many sparrows" (Luke 12:5, 7). Second, such warnings may be likened to a form of spiritual chemotherapy in which Jesus confronts us with a choice between life and death in order to shock us into battling the cancer of sin. Thus when Jesus describes the devastating consequences of sin, he does so knowing that he can provide a better alternative. Finally, as these first two factors imply, Jesus' warnings presuppose that the primary power for obedience is not fear *but the positive desire that lies behind it*: we fear death because we desire life; we fear sickness because we desire health; we fear loss because we desire gain. Jesus intends us to be repelled by the ugliness of sin and its eternally devastating effects, so that we will be drawn more powerfully to the beauty of our heavenly Father's goodness. In other words, the warnings of Luke's Gospel empower obedience not simply through fear, but by breaking our desire for sin and awakening our desire for God. As we will see in our next chapter, the cultivation of such desire is one of the keys to the practice of imitating Christ.

## Faith and Prayer

When we download new computer software, we're usually asked to check a box indicating that we've read a user agreement and that we accept its terms. This easily becomes a meaningless but obligatory ritual: we know we haven't read the agreement, but we also know we have to check the box if we want to get on with using the software. In a book like this, speaking of faith and prayer could feel like "checking the box"—these are topics we're obligated to mention, though we're more anxious to get on with more practical things. But according to Luke's Gospel, if we are to mature as disciples of Jesus, and therefore as imitators of Jesus, it is essential that we grow in faith, and in prayer as one of its chief expressions. In other chapters we have seen that Jesus' life is characterized by trust in God and by prayer, so that these may be classified as *marks* of Christlikeness. Here, though, we want to stress the fact that these marks are also *means*—sources of strength and power for growth in obedience to Christ, and therefore in likeness to him.

Two texts in Luke particularly stress the connection between faith and spiritual growth.

First, as mentioned earlier in this chapter, Luke 17:3–6 links forgiveness and faith: when Jesus requires forgiving a brother seven times in a day, the response of the apostles is, "Increase our faith!" Though Jesus redirects their request—what they need is not an *increase* of faith, since even "faith like a grain of mustard seed" is sufficient for powerful results—he does not dispute their assumption that the kind of forgiveness he demands will require a power that God alone can grant. Second, the account of the rich ruler in Luke 18:18–30 makes a similar point, though without the vocabulary of "faith." When the ruler refuses to give up everything to follow him, Jesus observes that it is unimaginably difficult for "those who have wealth to enter the kingdom of God!" (Luke 18:24). This makes Jesus' disciples wonder if it is possible for anyone to be saved, to which Jesus replies, "What is impossible with man is possible with God" (Luke 18:27). As these texts show, faith in God's redeeming power is necessary not only for initial salvation, but for the life of radical repentance and obedience to which Jesus calls us.[5]

5. Compare the Westminster Confession of Faith 14.2, which notes (1) that Christians act upon and yield obedience to Scripture's teaching *by faith*; and (2) that "saving faith" trusts Christ for *sanctification* as well as justification.

Having seen that faith is necessary for the kind of spiritual growth Jesus requires, we now need to say what faith is. Drawing on lessons learned from my colleague Dr. Hans Bayer, professor of New Testament at Covenant Theological Seminary, I would summarize it as follows: *faith is that confidence, bestowed on us by God's grace, and drawn out of us by his greatness, which makes us willing to entrust our whole selves to him.* By implication, *confidence in ourselves—confidence that turns inward to focus on our own worthiness—is contrary to faith.* This understanding of faith is particularly clear in Luke 7:1–10, where Jesus interacts with a Gentile centurion whose servant is dying:

- The centurion recognizes Jesus' greatness: "Lord . . . I am not worthy to have you come under my roof" (Luke 7:6).
- The centurion expresses profound confidence in Jesus' authority to heal, and thus entrusts his servant's life to Jesus: "But say the word, and let my servant be healed" (Luke 7:8).
- Unlike the Jewish leaders who tell Jesus that the centurion is "worthy" because of his character and deeds (Luke 7:4–5), the centurion mentions nothing that might qualify him to receive Jesus' mercy.
- Ultimately, Jesus commends the centurion: "I tell you, not even in Israel have I found such faith" (Luke 7:9).

If faith is necessary for spiritual growth, it must be a particular kind of faith, focused on divine greatness rather than on ourselves. Therefore growth in Christlikeness requires that we focus on the excellence of the one we imitate, and not on our ability as imitators.

A final text related to faith deserves mention because of its potential to encourage us as we pursue growth in Christlikeness.

In Luke 13:18–21, Jesus compares God's kingdom first to a mustard seed that grows and becomes a tree in whose branches the "birds of the air" make their nests, and then to a lump of leaven that works through a quantity of flour large enough to feed one hundred people. Clearly Jesus is calling us to trust God to bring about overwhelming results from beginnings that seem insignificant. While Jesus' words have application beyond individual spiritual growth, they offer us hope as we seek to imitate Christ. At times progress toward this goal will seem impossible, either because the goal itself is so lofty, or because we sense that we in our sin and weakness offer God so little to work with. But even at such times, we may trust that God is at work, enabling us to reflect more and more the image of his Son. The tree does not spring up overnight; the influence of the leaven is not immediate. But as our confidence in God's greatness grows, so shall our power for obedience, and ultimately our likeness to his Son.

If faith is a confidence granted by God's grace and drawn out of us by his greatness, prayer is a key expression of such confidence. According to the Lord's Prayer in Luke 11:2–4, prayer begins with a posture of reverence and dependence: God is our Father whose name is to be hallowed, a king whose reign is to be welcomed; and he is the only one who can supply our needs, forgive our sins, and deliver us from temptation. Prayer also acknowledges that God is more generous than a friend (Luke 11:5–8) and more loving than a human father (Luke 11:9–13). As children ask their fathers for food that gives them bodily strength, we may ask God for the gift of the Holy Spirit, who gives us strength for spiritual growth (Luke 11:13).

To confirm that prayer is one of the chief means by which we seek, and God supplies, spiritual strength, we may look to three features of Luke 22. First, Jesus indicates that he has prayed for Simon "that [his] faith may not fail" (Luke 22:32). Second, at Gethsemane Jesus prays for and receives strength to do God's will (Luke 22:41–44). Third, Jesus twice instructs his disciples to pray "that [they] may not enter into temptation" (Luke 22:40, 46). If God could provide sufficient strength for Jesus and his apostles in the events leading up to the crucifixion, surely he can empower us as we encounter obstacles to spiritual growth. Prayer is therefore not only a mark of Christlikeness, but a means through which God grants us the power of the Holy Spirit—the power for Christlike devotion to God, even in the face of hardship and temptation.

## Conclusion: Fuel and Fire

Suppose that you wanted to launch a heavy weight—roughly 4.5 million pounds—into outer space—straight up, opposite the pull of gravity. How would you do it? This is the challenge that faced NASA engineers who designed the space shuttle. Their solution involved two solid rocket boosters and an external fuel tank, holding a combined weight of over three million pounds of fuel. Needless to say, the chemistry, physics, and mechanical systems involved are staggeringly complex. Yet the most important component of the shuttle's launch system is a simple one: fire. Without fire—a process of combustion by which the energy stored in the fuel is released—the fuel would remain useless, and the shuttle would sit motionless on the launch pad.

You and I are like the space shuttle. We desire to soar, to break free of the gravity of sin so that we might grow as disciples of Jesus, trusting him as our Savior, obeying him as our Lord, and imitating him as our example. But unless there is fuel in our tanks, and fire to unleash its unimaginable power, we will never leave the launch pad. No matter how well we know the marks of Christlikeness, growth is impossible without the means by which they are produced and sustained. As we have learned in this chapter, however, we have access to both fuel and fire. Through Jesus, God has given us four sources of fuel for growth—a potent mix of repentance, forgiveness, and joy; the indicative-imperative relationship; the powerful discipline of warnings; along with faith and prayer—and he has given us the Holy Spirit, the fire that releases all of this transforming power into our lives. It is through these means that we will grow as imitators of Christ; what we must do to make the most of them is the subject of our concluding chapter.

# 14

# I Want to Be Like Jesus—Now What?

YOU ARE A FISHERMAN—not from the twenty-first century, but from Jesus' day. Like all of your family before you, you've been fishing for as long as you can remember; it's in your blood, in your very bones. And three things are true of you. First, no matter how long you fish, you will never be finished. You will never catch enough fish to say, "That's it! Now I can feed my family forever. I'll never have to worry about food or finances again!" Second, you are utterly dependent on something outside your control. You don't put the fish in the water; you don't make them grow big enough to eat; and, despite the good-natured boasts you exchange with friends, you can't guarantee there will be fish beneath your net when you cast it into the water. You will always depend on what God alone can provide. Third, you *never* sit in your boat and wait for fish to jump into your net! You repair boats, sharpen knives, untangle lines. You mend nets, cast them, haul them in. Though you depend on God, there are practical steps you must take in order to enjoy his provision.

So it is with the imitation of Christ. The desire to be like Jesus is "in the bones" of all who are his disciples. Because of the

Holy Spirit's work, we can't escape the core conviction expressed in an earlier chapter: *Deep reflection on Jesus' example, leading to sustained effort to be like him, is a central feature of the Christian life.*[1] Such deep reflection and sustained effort are not only central, they must be ongoing—for in this life, no matter how much we grow in likeness to Christ, we will never be finished. None of this suggests, however, that our growth as imitators of Christ is within our control; nothing short of God's supernatural power could enable sinful human beings to bear the image of his Son faithfully! Still, our dependence on God's grace doesn't entitle us to "sit in the boat" and wait for him to change us. Rather, there are practical steps we must take on the way to our goal. In this concluding chapter, we want to identify some of those steps. First, however, it will be helpful to review what we have learned so far.

## Looking Back: Three Key Features of the Imitation of Christ

To summarize what we've learned to this point, we may use the various components of the core conviction stated above:

- *Imitation as a central feature of the Christian life*: Chapters 1–2 argued that despite several weighty objections, the imitation of Christ deserves a prominent place in Christian thought and life.
- *Deep reflection on Jesus' example*: Chapters 3–4 offered careful reflection on two issues: Is Jesus the kind of person whose example can be imitated? And is Luke's Gospel the kind of document that calls readers to imitate Jesus' example? Chapters 5–12 then offered more detailed discussion of four major marks of likeness to Christ, first as

1. See chapter 2, p. 16.

seen in his life, and then as they might look in our lives: passion for the glory of God; passion for the good of others; willing denial of self; and patient endurance of hardship.

- *Sustained effort to be like Jesus*: Chapter 13, recognizing that it is not enough to identify the marks of likeness to Christ, focused on the means that will sustain our efforts to be like him. The following suggestions indicate where such efforts might begin.

## Looking Ahead: Three Practical Suggestions for Imitators of Christ

No fisherman who claims to know a foolproof way to catch a fish should be trusted. Similarly, I want to take care not to claim too much as I offer these practical suggestions, which remain useless apart from faith in Christ and the power of his Spirit. If we are trusting human effort or human wisdom to make us more like Jesus, we will be sorely disappointed. With this important truth in mind, we may now offer three answers to the question raised in the title of this chapter: "I want to be like Jesus—now what?"

### *1. If you want to be like Jesus, meditate on who he is and what he has done.*

If we hope to grow as imitators of Christ, there is no substitute for deep, prayerful reflection on his character and conduct—especially as depicted in Scripture, but also in the Lord's Supper.[2]

- *Meditate on Jesus and his work in Scripture*. Whether through reading Scripture or hearing it preached, we must learn

2. On the need to meditate on the Word of God, whether read or preached, see the Westminster Larger Catechism, Q. 157 and Q. 160, respectively. Question 174 affirms the need to meditate on Christ during the Lord's Supper.

of Jesus' example before we can follow it. Practical strategies for study of Scripture include the following: (1) for a day each week, or for a week each month, make one of the texts surveyed in chapter 2 a focus for study and prayer; (2) read through Matthew, Mark, or John, looking for one or more of the four marks of Christlikeness studied in this book; (3) meditate on one episode from the Gospels each day. Two benefits follow when we link our pursuit of Christlikeness to careful reflection on Scripture: first, we avoid the temptation to separate Christ's example from his work as Savior, which are always linked in the New Testament; second, we are never far removed from the themes of repentance, forgiveness, and the joy that accompanies salvation—without which imitation could become a crushing burden or a temptation to pride.[3]

- *Meditate on Jesus and his work in the Lord's Supper.* In Luke 22:24–27 and John 13:1–15, imitation of Jesus' example is closely connected with the institution of the Lord's Supper. When we celebrate this sacrament, therefore, gratitude for Jesus' saving death should be accompanied by a renewed commitment to imitating his self-sacrificial love and humble service.[4]

### *2. If you want to be like Jesus, pray with a focus on the marks and means of Christlikeness.*

Since Jesus himself relied so much on prayer, and since prayer is one of the chief means by which we experience spiritual growth, we should not presume that we can grow in likeness to

3. On the repentance-forgiveness-joy triad, see chapter 13, pp. 194-96.

4. For this connection, see John Calvin, *Institutes of the Christian Religion*, 2 vols., ed. John T. McNeill, The Library of Christian Classics, vol. 20 (Louisville, London, and Leiden: Westminster John Knox, 1960), 4.17.38–40.

him without seeking divine aid through prayer. But how might such prayers be shaped? The following suggestions and examples are based on our previous discussions of the marks (chapters 5–12) and means (chapter 13) of likeness to Christ:

- Pray for discernment, asking God to teach you how your life should express the marks of Christlikeness:
  - "Father, what are you calling me to do today to express passion for your glory as your Son did?"
  - "Lord, show me, through your Word, by your Spirit, by your providence in my daily circumstances, what it means for me to willingly deny myself."
- Pray with repentance, seeking God's forgiveness for failure to demonstrate the marks of Christlikeness:
  - "Father, Son, and Holy Spirit, forgive me for the ways I refuse to pursue the good of other people, and for the ways I pursue their good with less than wholehearted passion."
  - "Merciful God, it is difficult to patiently endure hardship. Forgive me for my sinful attempts to be like Jesus without surrendering my own comfort."
- Pray for enablement, asking God to transform you and sustain you through the means of Christlikeness:
  - "O God, apart from the power of your Holy Spirit, I cannot grow in likeness to your Son. Pour out your Spirit on me, that I may bear the image of Christ!"
  - "Lord Jesus, strengthen me to meet the costly demands of imitating you by giving me a clear vision of the costly sacrifice you made on my behalf."

- Pray with adoration, using the marks of Christlikeness to cultivate joy in Christ—and the strength that comes from joy:
    - "Jesus, my Redeemer—I stand in awe of the patience and gentleness you displayed in the midst of so many hardships, and especially at the cross. How I long to honor you by reflecting even a small measure of your endurance in my own life!"
    - "Father in heaven, there has never been a life more beautiful than that of your Son. What an unspeakable privilege—that the one who humbled himself and took up a cross to save sinners would allow me to take up a cross and follow him!"

Ultimately, there is no need to sharply separate the themes of discernment, repentance, enablement, and adoration in our prayers. But attention to each of these themes reminds us that there are many ways in which our confidence in God and our dependence on his provision need to grow.

***3. If you want to be like Jesus, spend time with other people who want to be like Jesus.***

According to the apostle Paul, God is conforming us "to the image of his Son, in order that he might be the firstborn among *many brothers*" (Rom. 8:29). In other words, God intends his children to grow to Christlike maturity in the context of family. Ideally, then, our personal growth as imitators of Christ will be seamlessly joined to growth we are experiencing together with our spiritual brothers and sisters. Several practices can help us in this regard:

- *Look for the theme of imitation when you worship with fellow believers.* Likeness to Christ is a pervasive theme in the worship of the church—even in traditions that typically neglect imitation as a doctrinal emphasis. While it is not the only theme to which we should be attuned in worship, we will find encouragement if we keep our eyes and ears open for the example of Christ as it is featured in song lyrics, prayers, Scripture readings, and sermons.

- *Meet regularly with other Christians who want to grow as imitators of Christ.* When I served as a pastor, I met regularly with a group of other pastors and teachers for prayer and encouragement. Eventually I noticed that our times together were increasing my passion for God *even when I was alone.* Similarly, the time we spend with other believers who long to grow in likeness to Christ will have deep and lasting impact. Whether informally or as part of a more structured ministry, and whether in groups of two, ten, or twenty, find others who seek such growth, and meet to pray, encourage one another, or study Scripture.

- *Meet regularly with a more mature Christian in whom you see evidence of Christlikeness.* As Scripture reminds us, it is helpful to imitate someone who is imitating Christ (1 Cor. 11:1). If you know someone who reflects the character of Christ, ask that person to meet with you for prayer, for meditation on Scripture, or for discussion of what it means to be a disciple of Jesus. Volunteer to assist such a person in a ministry about which he or she is passionate, so that you can observe Christlike character in action.

- *Read books that stimulate you to the biblical pursuit of Christlikeness.* The author of a book can be like a long-distance mentor, shaping us from another place, or even another time. For instance, we can no longer see John Bunyan's example of Christlike endurance of hardship—but we can read books by him and about him. For details on helpful (and some unhelpful) reading materials, see the list of "Select Resources for Reading and Study" on pages 225–28 below.

- *Disciple others in the biblical pursuit of Christlikeness.* All of us have a role to play in discipling others, whether our children, grandchildren, neighbors, or others God brings into our lives at different seasons. Many younger believers would greatly appreciate meeting together to learn more about Christlike character, whether by reading key biblical texts, by discussing a helpful book, or simply by sharing the daily challenges of life as a disciple of Jesus. Whatever the case may be, your own understanding of what it means to imitate Christ will deepen as you teach others.

As the author of Hebrews knew, God intends his people to "stir up one another to love and good works" (Heb. 10:24). If we want to grow as imitators of Christ, we will need to connect deeply and regularly with others so that we can stir each other up to the kind of love and good works that reflect the example of Jesus.

## Conclusion: Never Stop Starting

"Blessed is the man who never stops starting family devotions." I learned this piece of wisdom from one of my seminary professors. Of the many things I have said to people as a pastor and teacher, this has always been one of the best received. While women's contributions are vital to the spiritual health of a home, husbands and fathers have a particular responsibility to encourage the spiritual growth of their families through family worship and devotional practices. Yet, as many men can attest, it is easier to start such a practice than to continue it. Failed attempts pile up like so many discarded New Year's resolutions: "Let's read a chapter of Scripture together every day . . . Let's pray together for five minutes before breakfast . . . Let's work through this great new devotional book." Thus it is tremendously encouraging when a pastor or teacher reminds you that no matter how many times you have fallen down, you can stand up, dust yourself off, and start again: "Blessed is the man who *never stops starting*."

Likewise, the imitation of Christ is not an all-or-nothing affair. It is not something we begin in order to see how long we can maintain a perfect record, nor is it something we should put off until we think we can "get it right." Instead, it is a process of spiritual growth fueled by God's grace, enabled by the Holy Spirit's power, and undertaken at Jesus' command. But as the Gospels teach us, Jesus issues this command to flesh-and-blood human beings who are weak, imperfect, and capable of astounding acts of spiritual failure and forgetfulness. We will fall; but we can get up and start again, because this same Jesus has laid down his life to redeem us. Therefore, we must "never stop starting." And as we do, we will discover something: the *imitation of* Christ leads us to *intimacy with* Christ, because it focuses our attention on the one we love—the one who has loved us so perfectly.[5] Blessed, then, is anyone—man, woman, boy, or girl—who never stops starting to imitate Christ!

5. Adapted from William C. Spohn, *Go and Do Likewise: Jesus and Ethics* (New York: Continuum, 1999), 148–49.

# Questions for Study and Reflection

**Chapter 1—Why You Should *Not* Read This Book: Arguments against the Imitation of Christ**

1. Some people fear that stress on imitating Christ could undermine biblical teaching about Christ's work, and especially his death. What factors contribute to this fear (pp. 2–4?
2. What does it mean to say that the concept of imitation is hostile to grace or even Pelagian (pp. 4–6)?
3. Have you ever had the sense that imitating Christ is impossible (pp. 7–8)? If so, what led you to this conclusion?
4. Have any of the objections described in this chapter impacted the way you think and live? If so, how?

**Chapter 2—Why You *Should* Read This Book: Arguments for the Imitation of Christ**

1. Of the biblical texts surveyed in this chapter, which stand out to you as especially challenging, surprising, or encouraging? Why?
2. Summarize the four arguments given in this chapter in favor of the imitation of Christ.
3. How does the statement, "Abuse does not negate proper use," apply to the imitation of Christ (p. 18)? Give one example of abuse of imitation, and one example of proper use.

4. How might reflection on the imitation of Christ provide encouragement for despairing or discouraged Christians (p. 19)?
5. In what way does likeness to Christ represent a "triumph of divine grace" (pp. 19–20)? How does this answer the concern, stated in chapter 1, that imitation is hostile to grace?

### Chapter 3—Getting Oriented, Part I: Jesus as Son of God and Second Adam in Luke

1. Review the five themes featured in Luke's portrait of Jesus as the Son of God (pp. 23–25). How would our understanding of the imitation of Christ be impacted if we overemphasized these themes? If we neglected them?
2. In what two senses is Jesus "truly human" (p. 25)?
3. Briefly summarize the ways in which Luke portrays Jesus as the second Adam (pp. 26–31). How is Jesus like Adam? How is he unlike Adam?
4. Review the five themes featured in Luke's portrait of Jesus' humanity (pp. 31–32). How would our understanding of the imitation of Christ be impacted if we overemphasized these themes? If we neglected them?

### Chapter 4—Getting Oriented, Part II: Foundations for Studying Imitation in Luke

1. What lines of evidence indicate that Luke intends us to read his Gospel with the imitation of Jesus' example in mind (pp. 38–43)? Of these, which do you find most compelling? Why?
2. What does it mean to say that the descriptive texts in Luke's Gospel are not value neutral (p. 43)?
3. Summarize four guidelines that help us identify which features of Christ's life we are intended to imitate (pp. 43–48).

4. Why do we need an approach to imitating Christ that is "clear and simple"? Why must this approach also be "profound and comprehensive"? How does the compass metaphor illustrate this combination (pp. 49–51)?

**Chapter 5—Jesus' Passion for the Glory of God**

1. What is God's glory (pp. 53–4)?
2. Select one of the four key locations discussed in this chapter (pp. 57–67)—temple (Luke 2), wilderness (Luke 4), garden (Luke 22), or cross (Luke 23). What aspects of Jesus' behavior there are unique, and cannot be imitated? What aspects provide us with an example of passion for God's glory?
3. Summarize the Old Testament backgrounds of Luke 22:42 and Luke 23:46. How do these backgrounds change the way you understand Jesus' prayers (pp. 65–67)?
4. As you read this chapter, what feature of Jesus' passion for the glory of God stands out to you as most surprising, most encouraging, or most challenging? Why?

**Chapter 6—Imitating Jesus' Passion for the Glory of God**

1. When Jesus calls people "hypocrites," what does he mean (p. 70)? How does this impact the way you understand the sin of hypocrisy?
2. Review the three hypocritical tendencies and the three forms of idolatry discussed in this chapter (pp. 71–73). Give an example of how one of these might show up in our lives today, and of how we might combat it.
3. Discuss the statement, "Christlike passion for the glory of God involves the whole person loving the whole God." Against what dangers does this statement warn us (pp. 73–74)?

4. Summarize the distinction between *mission* and *vocation*. How does your current vocation give you opportunities to "imitate Christ by furthering his mission" (pp. 76–78)?
5. What does it mean to love God's presence (pp. 80–83)? Why is this so important?

**Chapter 7—Jesus' Passion for the Good of Others**

1. In your own words, summarize what the vocabulary of salvation implies (p. 89).
2. According to Luke's Gospel, from what does Jesus save us (pp. 89–94)? In your experience, how does this compare to the way many Christians understand salvation?
3. What two messages does Jesus send when he seeks "the lost" (pp. 94–95)? Why is it important to remember both of these truths?
4. What does it mean to say that Jesus seeks "the least" (pp. 95–97)?
5. Evaluate the following statement: Jesus' example teaches us that all Christians are called to martyrdom (pp. 100–101).

**Chapter 8—Imitating Jesus' Passion for the Good of Others**

1. Summarize some of the safeguards we must keep in mind when interpreting Jesus' miracles (pp. 104–5). What might result if we neglected these safeguards?
2. How might you answer someone who felt that imitating Jesus meant performing miracles, conquering death, or forgiving sins (pp. 106–7)?
3. What does it mean to engage in Christlike hospitality (pp. 108–12 )? How is this different from hospitality as it is understood in our culture?
4. What distinguishes Christlike accountability from rude, loveless attacks pp. 112–15)?

5. Summarize the range of needs to which Christlike compassion must respond (pp. 116–17). Which of these is easiest for you to neglect? For your church? For your culture?

**Chapter 9—Jesus' Willing Denial of Self**

1. What first comes to mind when you hear the term *self-denial*? Does it have positive or negative associations for you? Why?
2. In your own words, explain how Jesus' consistent embrace of his identity as God's Son is an expression of self-denial (pp. 124–26).
3. Describe some of the ways Jesus denied himself by rejecting human expectations for his ministry as Messiah (pp. 126–28).
4. Summarize what the image of cross-bearing would have suggested to Jesus' first hearers (pp. 129–30). How does this change the way you understand this aspect of discipleship?
5. In what ways is Jesus' call to a "downward-then-outward" model of servanthood more challenging than one that is outward only (pp. 131–33)? One that is downward only?

**Chapter 10—Imitating Jesus' Willing Denial of Self**

1. On pages 141–42 we saw an example of how dealing with temptation to sexual sin might require enduring loss and disgrace. Give another, similar example from daily life.
2. To what human resources are you tempted to look for salvation (pp. 142–43)?
3. Of the false standards of self-definition discussed in this chapter (pp. 144–50), which ones are most problematic for you? Why?
4. Among your peer group, what are some of the status markers that people use to put themselves "first" (p. 151)?

5. In what ways do you feel pressure to treat people as obstacles, competitors, or tools (p. 152)? How does the love of Christ enable you to resist this pressure?

### Chapter 11—Jesus' Patient Endurance of Hardship

1. In what ways does modern society promise us immunity to hardship and suffering (pp. 158–62)? How does this make it difficult to be content?
2. Name some specific details from Luke's Gospel that highlight Jesus' courage (pp. 162–64).
3. What example of Jesus' gentleness (pp. 165–69) do you find most deeply moving? Why?
4. How might you respond to someone who found some of Jesus' words and actions to be inappropriately angry, harsh, or vindictive (pp. 168–69)?
5. Describe the kind of situation in which you, like Jesus' apostles (pp. 170–71), feel quick to vengeance. How might you show Christlike compassion instead?

### Chapter 12—Imitating Jesus' Patient Endurance of Hardship

1. How have extreme perspectives on suffering (pp. 174–76) impacted you? What effect does a more balanced, biblical perspective have on your view of suffering?
2. What particular fears is Jesus' example currently calling you to face as you pursue God's will (p. 177)?
3. Discuss the difference between *hard words* and *humiliating words* (pp. 181–82). When are hard words appropriate? How might we know if we have crossed the line?
4. What are some of the hardships that God has called, or is calling, you to endure in order to show mercy to people in need (pp. 183–85)?

5. Who are some of the "slow learners" to whom God is calling you to extend mercy (pp. 185–86)? In what ways have you received mercy from God despite being a slow learner?

**Chapter 13—Fuel and Fire: How Real People Grow as Imitators of Christ**

1. Of the five means of Christlikeness, which do you find most encouraging, and why? Which do you most tend to neglect, and why?
2. In your own words, summarize the relationships among repentance, forgiveness, and joy (pp. 194–96). How does this triad motivate and empower our spiritual growth?
3. In your own words, summarize the "indicative-imperative" relationship reflected in Scripture (pp. 196–98).
4. What three arguments suggest that fear is not the primary motivation for obedience (pp. 199–200)?
5. What is faith, and what is its opposite (pp. 200–3)? Based on this understanding, why is faith necessary for growth in Christlikeness?

**Chapter 14—I Want to Be Like Jesus—Now What?**

1. Based on the suggestions in this chapter (pp. 209–10), identify two or three concrete ways that God is calling you to meditate on who Christ is and what he has done. Share these with someone who can encourage you in this discipline.
2. Based on the suggestions in this chapter (pp. 210–12), write some sample prayers or a list of prayer topics that would help you focus on the marks and means of Christlikeness.
3. For the next month, keep a journal noting how the theme of imitation is featured in the worship services you attend (pp. 212–13).
4. Through prayerful reflection, identify other people—including a more mature mentor—with whom you might

spend time in order to focus on growth in Christlikeness (pp. 213–14). Work out a schedule for meeting together over the next one to three months, and decide together whether you would like to focus on prayer, Scripture study, reading a book, or some combination.

# Select Resources for Reading and Study

## Resources for Devotional Reading

Calvin, John. *Institutes of the Christian Religion*. 2 vols. Edited by John T. McNeill. Translated by Ford Lewis Battles. The Library of Christian Classics, vols. 20–21. Louisville, London, and Leiden: Westminster John Knox, 1960. See Calvin's discussion of the Christian life in book 3, chapters 7–8.

Edwards, Jonathan. "A Treatise Concerning Religious Affections, in Three Parts." In vol. 1 of *The Works of Jonathan Edwards*, 236–343. 2 vols. Edinburgh and Carlisle, PA: Banner of Truth, 1974. Section 8 addresses "the Christian spirit," which is modeled on Christ's example.

Flavel, John. *The Works of John Flavel*. 6 vols. Reprint, London: Banner of Truth Trust, 1968. See 1:223–45 and 2:397–421: sermons on Phil. 2:8 and on the imitation of Christ as a mark of the true believer, respectively.

Murray, Andrew. *Like Christ: Thoughts on the Blessed Life of Conformity to the Son of God*. Chicago: Revell, 1895. Arranged in 31 chapters for a one-month devotional study. Available free, though with many typographical errors, at http://www.worldinvisible.com/library/murray/like_christ.

Warfield, B. B. *The Person and Work of Christ*. Edited by Samuel G. Craig. Philadelphia: Presbyterian and Reformed, 1950. Warfield's sermon, "Imitating the Incarnation," is included as an appendix to the book.

## Resources for Personal Study

Allen, Michael. "Imitating Jesus." *Modern Reformation* 18, 2 (March/April 2009): 27–30.

Berkouwer, G. C. *Faith and Sanctification*. Translated by John Vriend. Studies in Dogmatics. Grand Rapids: Eerdmans, 1952. See chapter 7, "The Imitation of Christ."

Griffiths, Michael. *The Example of Jesus*. The Jesus Library. Downers Grove, IL: InterVarsity Press, 1985.

Hardin, Leslie T. *The Spirituality of Jesus: Nine Disciplines Christ Modeled for Us*. Grand Rapids: Kregel, 2009.

Issler, Klaus. *Living into the Life of Jesus: The Formation of Christian Character*. Downers Grove, IL: InterVarsity Press, 2012.

Longenecker, Richard N., ed. *Patterns of Discipleship in the New Testament*. McMaster New Testament Studies. Grand Rapids and Cambridge: Eerdmans, 1996.

Miller, Paul E. *Love Walked among Us: Learning to Love Like Jesus*. Colorado Springs: NavPress, 2001.

Shuster, Marguerite. "The Use and Misuse of the Idea of the Imitation of Christ." *Ex Auditu* 14 (1998): 70–81.

Sider, Ronald J. *Living Like Jesus: Eleven Essentials for Growing a Genuine Faith*. Grand Rapids: Baker, 1996.

Stalker, Rev. James. *Imago Christi: The Example of Jesus Christ*. New York: Hunt & Eaton, 1894. A well-known older resource that at some points goes beyond Scripture, and at some points captures biblical truth powerfully.

Swindoll, Charles R. *So, You Want to Be Like Christ? Eight Essentials to Get You There*. Nashville: W Publishing Group, 2005.

Wilkins, Michael J. *Following the Master*. Grand Rapids: Zondervan, 1992. See especially chapter 7, "Becoming Like Jesus."

———. *In His Image: Reflecting Christ in Everyday Life*. Colorado Springs: NavPress, 1997.

## Resources for Advanced Study

à Kempis, Thomas. *The Imitation of Christ*. Translated by Aloysius Croft and Harold Bolton. Milwaukee: Bruce, 1940. Available free at http://www.ccel.org/ccel/kempis/imitation.html. While some aspects of à Kempis's teaching are hard to reconcile with biblical truth, discerning readers can glean much from this fifteenth-century devotional classic, which emphasizes patient endurance of hardship for Christ's sake, and the necessity of God's grace for growth in holiness.

Adam, A. K. M. *Faithful Interpretation: Reading the Bible in a Postmodern World*. Minneapolis: Fortress, 2006. Chapter 6, "Walk This Way: Repetition, Difference, and the Imitation of Christ," identifies several dangers of an imitation ethic, and gives a brief but powerful critique of Sheldon's *In His Steps* and the WWJD movement.

Burridge, Richard A. *Imitating Jesus: An Inclusive Approach to New Testament Ethics*. Grand Rapids and Cambridge: Eerdmans, 2007. Written from a moderately critical perspective.

Capes, David B. "*Imitatio Christi* and the Gospel Genre." *Bulletin for Biblical Research* 13, 1 (2003): 1–19.

Foster, Richard J., and Gayle D. Beebe. *Longing for God: Seven Paths of Christian Devotion*. Downers Grove, IL: InterVarsity Press, 2009. Pages 141–48 provide an excellent introduction to Thomas à Kempis's *The Imitation of Christ*.

Gorman, Michael J. *Cruciformity: Paul's Narrative Spirituality of the Cross*. Grand Rapids and Cambridge: Eerdmans, 2001.

Hays, Richard B. "A Discussion: Richard Burridge's Jesus. Response to Richard Burridge, *Imitating Jesus*." *Scottish Journal of Theology* 63, 3 (2010): 331–35.

Johnson, Luke Timothy. *Living Jesus: Learning the Heart of the Gospel*. New York: HarperCollins, 1999.

Malatesta, Edward, ed. *Imitating Christ*. Religious Experience Series 5. St. Meinrad, IN: Abbey Press, 1974. A multiauthor work summarizing Roman Catholic viewpoints.

McGrath, Alister. "In What Way Can Jesus Be a Moral Example for Christians?" *Journal of the Evangelical Theological Society* 34, 3 (September 1991): 289–98.

Miles, Margaret R. "Imitation of Christ: Is It Possible in the Twentieth Century?" *Princeton Seminary Bulletin* 10, 1 (March 1989): 7–22.

Smith, Gary Scott. "Charles M. Sheldon's *In His Steps* in the Context of Religion and Culture in Late Nineteenth Century America." *Fides et historia* 22, 2 (Summer 1990): 47–69.

Sheldon, Charles M. *In His Steps*. New York: Grosset & Dunlap, 1935. A best-selling novel built around the question, "What would Jesus do?" Features little serious reflection on the Gospels, and contains only passing references to Jesus' saving work.

Spencer, F. Scott. "Imitation of Jesus." In *Dictionary of Scripture and Ethics*, ed. Joel B. Green, 397–99. Grand Rapids: Baker, 2011.

———. *What* Did *Jesus Do? Gospel Profiles of Jesus' Personal Conduct*. Harrisburg, PA: Trinity Press International, 2003.

Spohn, William C. *Go and Do Likewise: Jesus and Ethics*. New York: Continuum, 1999.

Stegman, Thomas. *The Character of Jesus: The Linchpin to Paul's Argument in 2 Corinthians*. Rome: Pontificio Istituto Biblico, 2005.

Tinsley, E. J. *The Imitation of God in Christ: An Essay on the Biblical Basis of Christian Spirituality*. London: SCM Press, 1960.

———. "Some Principles for Reconstructing a Doctrine of the Imitation of Christ." *Scottish Journal of Theology* 25, 1 (February 1972): 45–57.

van Keulen, Dirk. "Herman Bavinck on the Imitation of Christ." *Scottish Bulletin of Evangelical Theology* 29, 1 (Spring 2011): 78–91.

Watson, Francis. "A Discussion: Richard Burridge's Jesus. Can the Historical Jesus Teach Ethics? In response to Richard Burridge, *Imitating Jesus*." *Scottish Journal of Theology* 63, 3 (2010): 331–35.

Webster, John B. "The Imitation of Christ." *Tyndale Bulletin* 37 (1986): 95–120. A thorough, balanced presentation of both the dangers and the necessity of imitation.

# Index of Scripture

# Index of Subjects and Names